ALL
GOD'S
COMFORT

To Pumpkin
Love Dad

ALL
GOD'S
COMFORT

HERBERT
LOCKYER

WHITAKER
HOUSE

Unless otherwise indicated, all Scripture quotations are taken from the King James Version of the Holy Bible. Scripture quotations marked (NIV) are taken from the *Holy Bible, New International Version*®, NIV®, © 1973, 1978, 1984 by the International Bible Society. Used by permission of Zondervan. All rights reserved. Scripture quotations marked (NASB) are taken from the *New American Standard Bible*®, NASB ®, © 1960, 1962, 1963, 1968, 1971, 1972, 1973, 1975, 1977, 1988 by The Lockman Foundation. Used by permission. (www.Lockman.org). Scripture quotations marked (NKJV) are taken from the *New King James Version*, © 1979, 1980, 1982, 1984 by Thomas Nelson, Inc. Used by permission. All rights reserved. Scripture quotations marked (RV) are taken from the Revised Version of the Holy Bible. Scripture quotations marked (SCOFIELD) are taken from the Scofield Reference Bible, © 1963, Oxford University Press. Scripture quotations marked (MOFFATT) are taken from *The Bible: A New Translation*, © 1922, 1924, 1925, 1926, 1935, by Harper & Row, Publishers, Inc., © 1950, 1952, 1953, 1954, by James A. R. Moffatt. Scripture quotations marked (AMP) are taken from *The Amplified*® *Bible*, © 1954, 1958, 1962, 1964, 1965, 1987 by The Lockman Foundation. Used by permission. (www.Lockman.org).

Boldface type in the Scripture quotations indicates the author's emphasis.

All God's Comfort

ISBN: 978-1-62911-351-7
eBook ISBN: 978-1-62911-352-4
Printed in the United States of America
© 2015 Ardis A. Lockyer

Whitaker House
1030 Hunt Valley Circle
New Kensington, PA 15068
www.whitakerhouse.com

Library of Congress Cataloging-in-Publication Data (Pending)

1 2 3 4 5 6 7 8 9 10 11 **ЛJ** 22 21 20 19 18 17 16 15

CONTENTS

PREFACE

One of the marvels of the Bible is the profitable way in which it touches life at all its points. All who suffer discomfort or fear for any reason must be guided by the God of all comfort.

> *Praise be to the God and Father of our Lord Jesus Christ, the Father of compassion and the God of all comfort, who comforts us in all our troubles, so that we can comfort those in any trouble with the comfort we ourselves have received from God. For just as the sufferings of Christ flow over into our lives, so also through Christ our comfort overflows. If we are distressed, it is for your comfort and salvation; if we are comforted, it is for your comfort, which produces in you patient endurance of the same sufferings we suffer. And our hope for you is firm, because we know that just as you share in our sufferings, so also you share in our comfort.* (2 Corinthians 1:3–7 NIV)

In our complex lives today, the need to know God's comfort is more necessary than ever. It does not require deep insight to discern the similarity between the decadent condition of human society in the days of Noah and the moral degeneracy of our age some six thousand years later.

> *Now the earth was corrupt in God's sight and was full of violence.*
> (Genesis 6:11 NIV)

Did not our Lord Himself prophesy that as it was in the days of Noah, so shall it be in the latter days of world history? No matter where we turn in our times,

> *Men's hearts failing them for fear, and for looking after those things which are coming on the earth....But as the days of Noah were, so shall also the coming of the Son of man be.*
>
> (Luke 21:26; Matthew 24:37)

Even today, men's hearts are failing them because of the grievous things happening on the earth.

What wickedness prevails! Think of the defiant lawlessness, unrestrained violence, vandalism, destruction, terrorism, hijackings, drug and alcohol addiction, killings, robberies, and corruption (in morals, business, and politics). Consider wars, with their lust for power, uprooting thousands of frightened souls. Look at national catastrophic events such as invasions by enemies, earthquakes, floods, railway and plane disasters, as they leave behind a multitude of broken hearts and broken homes. Consider also financial bankruptcy (nationally, communally, and personally), loose views of marriage with opposite sexes living together, and abortion with its murder of unborn children. All add to the corruption of our age.

In such a welter of godlessness the question often arises, "What is the greatest need of such a time as this?" According to one's outlook upon and assessment of society, various answers are forthcoming. The purpose of this book is to indicate that one of the most pressing needs of this hour is the preaching and practice of *comfort*, to combat the ever-increasing fear causing so many hearts to fail. It was to a sinful and sinning nation, who received double for all its sins, this divine message came: "*Comfort ye, comfort ye my people, saith your God*" (Isaiah 40:1). An ever-increasing number are distressed, distraught, disillusioned, and disappointed. They are in sad need of someone to soothe and sympathize, to console and encourage. May God raise up an ever-growing army of comforters who believe the time to comfort is when sorrow is written on the bosom of the earth.

God, who created us, knows our every need. God comforts us when we are cast down and sent His Son to bind up the brokenhearted and to teach good news to the poor. (See Isaiah 61:1.) God also gave us the Holy Spirit, the Comforter who abides with us forever. (See John 14:16.)

This book is written to help the reader find the true source of comfort and to be able to sing with David:

May your unfailing love be my comfort, according to your promise to your servant. Let your compassion come to me that I may live, for your law is my delight. (Psalm 119:76–77 NIV)

Almighty and Everlasting God,
The Comfort of the sad;
The strength of the sufferer;
Let the prayers of those that cry
Out of tribulation, come unto Thee;
That all may rejoice, to find
That Thy mercy is present
With them in their afflictions;
Through Jesus Christ our Lord,
Amen.

PART I

COMFORT IS A DIVINE VIRTUE

1

COMFORT, A DIVINE VIRTUE

Christ the Comforter: *"The Lord Jesus Christ Himself...comfort your hearts"* (2 Thessalonians 2:16–17).

The Holy Spirit, Divine Comforter: *"The comfort of the Holy Spirit"* (Acts 9:31 NASB).

Comfort from the Scriptures: *"Through comfort of the scriptures* [we] *might have hope"* (Romans 15:4).

Comfort by Angels: *"The angel...talked with me with good words and comfortable words"* (Zechariah 1:13).

Comfort by Christians: *"The son of consolation"* (Acts 4:36).

Comfort in Death: *"[Lazarus] died....Now he is comforted"* (Luke 16:22, 25).

What does the Bible actually mean by the term comfort? The word, with all its shades of meaning, appears 128 times in the Bible, 67 in the Old Testament and 61 in the New Testament. The Greek word for comfort, with all its descriptive forms and declensions, means:

+ A calling; to summon to one's side; entreaty.

+ To speak kindly, soothingly, with tenderness.

+ Consolation; to persuade.

+ To cheer up, be of good courage, be animated.

+ To soothe, speak tenderly, pacify.

+ To exhort, console—the same form used in medications that help irritation, as in 2 Corinthians 7:5–7:

For even when we came into Macedonia our flesh had no rest, but we were afflicted on every side: conflicts without, fears within. But God, who comforts the depressed, comforted us by the coming of Titus; and not only by his coming, but also by the comfort with which he was comforted in you, as he reported to us your longing, your mourning, your zeal for me; so that I rejoiced even more.

(NASB)

The English word *comfort* comes from an Old English root meaning "to strengthen" and implies physical or mental refreshment of an active kind—an invigoration. Consolation may suggest a softer kind of mental refreshment. The term also implies the influence of an animating sermon (see Acts 9:31), where emphasis is upon the instrument used, the preaching or speaking with which the preacher persuades and soothes. (See 2 Corinthians 13:11.) In Matthew 9:22, we have the thought of a consolation as an exhortation, invitation, warning, or entreaty.

Another word for comfort indicates a kind, soothing, persuasive approach, and is suggestive of more tenderness than the previous meaning. It is connected with consolation in sorrow. (See John 11:19, 31; Colossians 4:11.) Most of the references, however, imply its pacifying, persuasive ministry. Still, a further original word meaning carries the idea of good spirits, animation, and to be of good courage. It was this word Paul used to hearten his fellow voyagers during the terrific storm at sea: *"I exhort you to be of good cheer"* (Acts 27:22). Cheer up, take heart, feel confident also describes the use of comfort in Matthew 9:22 and Philippians 2:19.

Consolation, occurring some seventeen times in the King James Version, is often given as *comfort* in the Revised Version, seeing that the two words convey similar meanings, and are, therefore, interchangeable. (See 2 Corinthians 1:3, 7; Acts 15:31.) The Greek word used for *consolation* also denotes comforter (see John 14:16) and implies relief in distress or depression. (See Jeremiah 1:7–8.)

In the same section where Isaiah speaks of God comforting His children as a mother consoles her offspring, he also says God's people *"will nurse and be satisfied at her comforting breasts; you will drink deeply and delight in her overflowing abundance"* (Isaiah 66:11 NIV). Truly, divine comfort comes in many guises! Both divine and human channels convey these consolations to our needy hearts. *"In the multitude of my thoughts within me thy comforts delight my soul"* (Psalm 94:19). *"Whence shall I seek comforters for thee?"* (Nahum 3:7). Happily, God has provided us with many comforters.

CHRIST THE COMFORTER

Matthew Roydon, who died in 1622, composed a moving elegy for his friend Sir Philip Sidney, the renowned English poet, statesman, and soldier of the last half of the sixteenth century. Roydon wrote of him as having,

> A sweet attractive kind of grace,
> A full assurance given by looks,
> Continual comfort in a face,
> The lineaments of Gospel books;
> I trow that countenance cannot lie,
> Whose thoughts are legible in the eye.
> But eyes and ears, and ev'ry thought;
> Were with his sweet perfections caught.

Continual comfort in a face! Is this not truer of the face of Jesus, who was marred more than any other man? His benign countenance, loving eyes, gracious presence, and heartfelt messages all exuded comfort. Touched with the feeling of our infirmities and sorrows, He could console as no other could. Did He not declare, *"I and the Father are one"* (John 10:30 NIV)? His Father revealed Himself as the God of all comfort, and the Son was closely united with the Father in such a virtue, seeing He came *"to comfort all that mourn"* (Isaiah 61:22; Corinthians 1:3). This is why we pray,

> Be with me when no other friend
> The mystery of my heart can share;
> And be Thou known, when fears transcend,
> By Thy best name of Comforter.
> —*Rawson*

The apostle Paul magnified God the Son as being just as consoling as God the Father: *"May our Lord Jesus Christ himself and God our Father, who loved us and by his grace gave us eternal encouragement and good hope, encourage you hearts and strengthen you in every good deed and word"* (2 Thessalonians 2:16–17 NIV).

Christ's comforting presence and consoling words and works permeate the Gospels, where He is found breaking up funerals, drying tears, raising the dead, healing lepers, casting out devils, dying for a world of sinners lost and ruined by the fall. What a divine Comforter He was—and ever is! One of His beatitudes reads, *"Blessed are they that mourn: for they shall be comforted"* (Matthew 5:4). The afflicted woman, diseased for twelve years, was one who knew experientially what is was to be comforted by Him. Touching the hem of His garment, she was healed. After she identified herself to Jesus, He greatly encouraged her by saying, *"Daughter, be of good comfort; thy faith hath made thee whole"* (Matthew 9:22).

The word Jesus used for comfort meant to be courageous of heart, cheer up, and feel confident! Can we not imagine how this believer in Jesus' omnipotence returned home with a spring in her step and a song in her heart? By faith, she had appropriated her share in *"the consolation of Israel"* (Luke 2:25).

> Jesus, all our consolations
> Flow from Thee, the sovereign good;
> Love, and faith, and hope, and patience,
> All are purchased by Thy blood;

Nor Thy richest grace impart,
Sanctify and fill the heart.
—*Author Unknown*

The most sublime reference, however, to the Master's influence as a comforter is found in His heartening message to His own disciples as He announced He was about to return to heaven: *"I will not leave you comfortless; I will come to you"* (John 14:18 SCOFIELD). But he came again to them in the person of another divine Comforter: *"I will pray the Father, and he shall give you another Comforter, that he may abide with you for ever…When the Comforter is come, whom I will send unto you from the Father"* (John 14:16; 15:26).

Two connected words in our Lord's parting promise deserve our attention, namely, *another* and *comforter*. First of all, consider the adjective, *another*, which has two distinct yet opposite meanings:

1. One of the same kind.

2. One of a different, distinct kind, separate from the first aspect, not the same.

It was the first idea that our Lord conveyed when He spoke of another comforter. The Holy Spirit would be the same in every way as the Comforter who was about to leave His disciples. Jesus could say, *"He that hath seen me hath seen the Father"* (John 14:9). Father and Son were absolutely identical in every way. In effect, it is also true, one that knows the Spirit and has seen Him at work, sees the Son, for the Spirit is the replica of the Son. Thus, the Comforter to come would be the same in every way as the Comforter about to depart—and what a comfort this blessed truth has been to the saints through the ages!

The term *comforter* is given as *advocate* or *helper* in the margin of the Revised Version. In 1 John 2:1, where John speaks of Christ as *"an advocate with the Father,"* the margin gives *comforter*. In Scripture, a *paraclete*, the Greek term for *comforter*, is an intercessor, a capable helper in time of need, or a person called to the side of another to aid them.

A certain missionary was struggling with the language of the natives among whom he labored. When he came to "advocate" in John 14:16, he tried to translate it into a word or phrase expressing the meaning to the native mind but was baffled. Calling to his native assistant, he said, "Come over to my side and help me with this word." Thus, all at once, the missionary had his translation: "one called alongside to help."

During His earthly ministry, Jesus had been God's advocate with men, pleading God's cause with them, seeking to win them for His Father. He was ever at the call of saint and sinner alike that needed His help. He was going away however, and both He and the Father would see to it that their own would not be left without another advocate on the earth.

This further heavenly comforter would not be recognized by an unspiritual world, but all true believers would know and welcome Him.

> *And I will ask the Father, and He will give you another Helper, that He may be with you forever....After a little while the world will no longer see Me, but you will see Me; because I live, you will live also....These things I have spoken to you while abiding with you. But the Helper, the Holy Spirit, whom the Father will send in My name, He will teach you all things, and bring to your remembrance all that I said to you.* (John 14:16, 19, 25–26 NASB)

> *When the Helper comes, whom I will send to you from the Father, that is the Spirit of truth who proceeds from the Father, He will testify about Me.* (John 15:26 NASB)

> *But I tell you the truth, it is to your advantage that I go away; for if I do not go away, the Helper will not come to you; but if I go, I will send Him to you.* (John 16:7 NASB)

Although the Holy Spirit came and took Christ's office on earth and has ever continued to serve the church and the world as Christ did while among men, Jesus is still the Advocate in heaven where He makes intercession for sinners, pleading their cause with God. (See Romans 8:34; 1 John 2:1.) As the Sankey hymn has it, "I have a Savior, He's pleading in glory."

THE HOLY SPIRIT, DIVINE COMFORTER

All this I have spoken while still with you. But the Counselor, the Holy Spirit, whom the Father will send in my name, will teach you all things and will remind you of everything I have said to you. Peace I leave with you; my peace I give you. I do not give to you as the world gives. Do not let your hearts be troubled and do not be afraid.   (John 14:25–27 NIV)

When the Counselor comes, whom I will send to you from the Father, the Spirit of truth who goes out from the Father, he will testify about me.   (John 15:26 NIV)

Now I am going to him who sent me, yet none of you asks me, "Where are you going?" Because I have said these things, you are filled with grief. But I tell you the truth: It is for your good that I am going away. Unless I go away, the Counselor will not come to you; but if I go, I will send Him to you.   (John 16:5–7 NIV)

Referring to His complete identification with His Father in nature and works, Jesus could say, "I and the Father are one." He could have likewise affirmed, "I am the Holy Spirit are one, for the Gospels reveal a holy intimacy between Jesus and the diving Spirit. Jesus' use of the phrase, "I...by the Spirit of God" (Matthew 12:28), must not be limited to the casting out of demons recorded in the narrative for it applies to our Lord's every action. He lived and walked in the Spirit, and all Jesus taught about the Spirit's actuality and activities was the natural outcome of the most blessed and harmonious fellowship between these two members of the Godhead. A word or two is therefore necessary as to the ministry of the Holy Spirit in the life of Jesus. The fine flour, unleavened (Jesus), was mingled with oil (the Spirit).

First, in His incarnation, our Lord emptied himself or stripped Himself of the insignia of majesty. He became subject to the Father's will and lived His life in the realm of that will. He likewise became dependent upon the life-giving Holy Spirit who was the One responsible for

Jesus becoming a man (see Luke 1:35) and who imparted to Him His full empowerment in all His preaching and teaching.

Second, in the days of His flesh, the Holy Spirit seemed to have labored exclusively with Jesus. The Holy Spirit concentrated all energies on Jesus as He went about doing good and healing all who were oppressed of the devil. (See Acts 10:38.) After Jesus' wondrous birth by the Spirit, there is no reference to the Spirit's association with any other individual until after His resurrection when Jesus said, *"Receive ye the Holy Ghost"* (John 20:22). John could say, *"The Holy Ghost was not yet given"* (John 7:39). There had to be a Man both able and willing to receive the Spirit in all fullness such as He did at Pentecost. For the first time in Jesus, Man was able to receive the Holy Spirit in entirety.

The authority of immediate knowledge of all aspects of truth, then, wedded to the power of the Holy Spirit, gave the teachings of Jesus an original element. Thus, prominent among His disciples was the personal leadership of the Spirit in the individual and corporate life of Christianity. (See John 14:26.) Jesus recognized that His purposes of salvation would be accomplished through the power of the Holy Spirit bringing home to the consciences of individuals the import of the preached words of Jesus. It was the Spirit who enlightened the minds of our Lord's auditors and brought to fruition a full harvest from the seeds of truth. In fact, when Jesus commenced His public ministry that Sabbath in the synagogue of Nazareth, it was with the recognition of the power and work of the Holy Spirit in His life, works, and teachings. (See Luke 4:18–19.)

> In us Abba, Father! cry;
> Earnest of our bliss on high;
> Seal of Immortality, Comforter Divine.

The fact of the leadership of the Spirit in the life of Jesus is stressed in the accounts of His temptation after His baptism in terms like *"led up of the Spirit"* (Matthew 4:1), *"the spirit driveth him"* (Mark 1:12), *"in the power of the Spirit"* (Luke 4:14), and God gave His Son the Spirit *"not…by measure"* (John 3:34).

Jesus could speak of Himself as Him whom God had sealed, and since it is by the Spirit of God that we are sealed, we remember the forecast of John the Baptist that Jesus would come as the Baptizer in the Holy Spirit. (See Ephesians 4:30; John 6:27.) The Spirit's ascent upon Jesus attested or sealed the Father's approval of His Son and gave great value to His teaching, not only about the Spirit, but about every other topic. Because of His own baptism with the Spirit by the Father, Jesus had the authority and ability to baptize in the Spirit. (See Matthew 3:11; John 1:33.) It must be observed that the Gospels never speak about the baptism *of* the Holy Spirit but always in or with the Spirit, the element in whom we are baptized.

Dr. W. Graham Scroggie suggests that the chief source of Christ's teaching on the Holy Spirit is His upper room discourse and the continuance of it on the way to Gethsemane (see John 14–16), and then he gives an outline of what Christ taught in His conversation with His own. But as there are valuable references to the Spirit's ministry in the other three Gospels, which John does not mention, these too must be brought into the Master's overall teaching on such an important theme. The following features are unmistakably plain.

A Person. To Jesus, the Holy Spirit was no mere influence or force or emanation from God but was a real Person as He Himself was, only without a visible body as Jesus had. All the elements of personality were His. For instance, terms of personality of the Spirit were continuously employed by Jesus. Pronouns like *He, Him,* and *Himself* are used frequent throughout the Gospels. (See Mark 12:36.) Count up the personal pronouns Jesus used of the Spirit in John 14:16–17, 26; 15:26; 16:7–8, 13–14, and you will conclude that our fellowship is not with *something* but with *Someone,* not with an exertion of divine energy but with a Person of the Trinity, not with an *it* but with *Him.* The RV gives *Him* for *it* in Romans 8:16, 26. True spiritual worship is dependent upon belief in the Spirit's personality.

Further, the qualities and operations of personality were attributed to the Holy Spirit by Jesus in His revelation of Him. The Spirit can teach, reveal, and communicate truth. (See John 14:26; 16:13.) The Spirit can lead, receive, glorify, speak, announce, and assist. (See John 14:16, 26; 15:26; 16:13–15; Mark 13:11.)

The Spirit can impart joy and gladness. That Jesus Himself was anointed with the oil of gladness is evident from Luke's account of the feelings of Jesus when the seventy returned from their mission and reported what mighty things had been accomplished. (See Psalm 45:7; Hebrews 1:9.) *"In that hour Jesus rejoiced in spirit"* (Luke 10:21). Weymouth translates the phrase, "At that hour Jesus was filled by the Holy Spirit with a rapturous joy." Paul reminds us that *"the fruit of the Spirit is…joy"* (Galatians 5:22–23), and the Spirit was the source of our Lord's joy and is likewise the One who inspires us to be glad in the Lord. Twice over, Jesus declared His joy was fulfilled in His disciples. Because of His inner fount of joy in the Spirit, Jesus carried no forbidding countenance but had a somewhat gracious and attractive person, drawing all classes, even children, to Him. Do we know what it is to have joy in God by the Spirit who indwells us? (See John 14:16–17.)

Further, Jesus believed not only in the personality of the Holy Spirit, but also in His deity. Had He not been the third Person of the blessed Trinity, the Spirit could never have accomplished the works ascribed to Him by Jesus. Only a divine Person can convict men of sin, regenerate the sinner's heart, cast out demons, and judge Satan. Jesus plainly states that associations of deity were the Spirit's (see Matthew 28:18–19; John 14:16, 26; 16:14–15), attributes of deity were His (see John 14:17, 26; 16:7, 12–13; Luke 2:26–27), and actions of deity were and continue to be His (see John 3:5; 16:8–14; Luke 4:1; 12:12).

As to the character of the Spirit, the same is indicated in the various titles Jesus used of Him, each of which carries its own significance.

Spirit of Truth (John 14:17; 16:13). The Holy Spirit inspired holy men to understand the truth, and then sent it forth. But the Spirit is not only the Revealer of truth, but a constant Witness to it. (See John 15:26–27; 16:12–13.) The receptive and teachable minds of the apostles found their impression of the truths Jesus taught quickened by the Holy Spirit. He had promised the enlightening of the Spirit to lead His followers into a larger appreciation of His gospel. (See John 14:26.) Promises of the future light and leadership of the Spirit had to be coupled, however, with obedience to qualify them for increased gifts of revelation. Jesus believed His disciples would remember the truth He taught them and that this truth would greatly extend the influence of His teaching through the enlightenment, illustrative presence, and leadership of the Spirit of truth who would specially empower the immature church after Pentecost. Thus, all the books of the New Testament became possible under the direct guidance of this selfsame Spirit. (See 1 Peter 1:11–12; 2 Peter 1:21.) What delight we experience when the Spirit of truth brings to our remembrance so many of the beautiful truths Jesus taught.

Holy Spirit (John 14:26; Luke 11:13). The Spirit is thus named one hundred times in Scripture under this title. *Ghost*, which is never used in the RV, is an old English word for spirit. The qualifying term *Holy* reminds us; not only of the Spirit's own inherent holiness, but also that the Spirit is the source of our holiness. "Be ye holy, even as I am holy"—such a command can only be realized as the Holy Spirit imparts divine holiness.

Spirit of Power (Luke 4:14, 18; 24:49; Acts 1:8; Romans 15:19). Power is the predominant feature of the Spirit's ministry, and such power is not *something* but *Someone*. Power is the manifestation of the Spirit's presence. This is evident in the life and work of Jesus. All the miracles of Jesus were performed through the Holy Spirit, especially the cure of demoniacs which was a conspicuous feature of the Master's miraculous ministry. The disciples were promised that power would be theirs as the Holy Spirit came upon them. Jesus knew their preparation to continue His ministry on earth would come by the empowerment of the Holy Spirit, and apostolic history reveals what the Spirit accomplished through the apostolate.

The Spirit's unceasing power is seen in the conviction of sin (see John 16:8; Acts 2:37), the regeneration of the sinner (see John 3:3, 5), and in the sanctification of the saved sinner (see John 17:17; 1 Corinthians 6:11; 1 Peter 1:2).

The Finger of God (Luke 11:20; Matthew 12:28). It is Luke, the beloved physician, who tells us that Jesus used the illustration of a finger to describe the Holy Spirit as a medium of power. Head, arm, and fingers are united in any action. The head plans and directs; then the strength of the arm through the fingers carries out the plan. How marvelously the fingers operate to carry out the dictates of the mind! The analogy resident in our Lord's symbol of the Spirit as the finger of God is apparent. God is the *Head*, Jesus is spoken of as the *Arm* of salvation, and the Spirit is the *Finger*, fulfilling the divine task both in the world (see John 16:8–11) and in the church (see John 14:26; 15:26; 16:12–15).

The Divine Comforter (John 14:16; 15:26). After announcing His coming departure from His own, Jesus exhorted the disciples not to be troubled in heart or mourn because of the coming separation. He would pray to the Father, and the Father would give them One like Himself to take His place. Jesus was careful to identify the coming comforter as the Spirit of truth and as the Holy Spirit. Such a title means an advocate, a pleader, a defender, and is transliterated *paraclete*, a term John applied to Jesus. (See 1 John 2:1; Romans 8:26.) Since Jesus had taught much about the Holy Spirit, it must have been assuring for the disciples to hear Him speak of the promised Comforter as the Spirit of your Father (see Matthew 10:20), the only time in Scripture He is thus named. Does such a title not imply that, like Jesus, the Spirit shares the care, concern, and compassion of the Father—the God of all comfort—for His children? Thus, the Comforter was to be like Jesus, represent Him in every way, and act as Jesus' other self.

The statement, "*It is expedient for you that I go away*" (John 16:7), must have perplexed the disciples. How could it be suitable for Jesus to leave them in a world of evil? Because of the limitations of His humanity, Jesus could not be in more than one place at a time. If comforting the saints in Bethany, He could not be in Galilee consoling His followers there. Now, by His Spirit, from whose presence none can flee (see Psalm 139:7), He is everywhere at the same time. Wherever there is a child of God in need, the Comforter is there to console, strengthen, and intercede. Truly, great is this mystery of our godliness! Thus, the mission of Jesus, commissioned by the Father, and empowered by the Holy Spirit, continued after the ascension and will only cease when the church is raptured at Christ's return.

Jesus recognized the unique ministry of the Holy Spirit, just as the early church lived under the impact of the Spirit's presence and presidency, when Jesus warned against ill-treating or despising the Holy Spirit, who has been called the Vicar of Christ. The reception hall of the temple, so suitable for preaching and teaching with all sorts of people having access to Jesus without the formalities of invitation, was the place where He uttered some of His most famous sayings and discourses. For instance, it was there that He refuted the calumny of the Jewish rulers and declared their blasphemy against the Holy Spirit. (See Matthew 12:31–32; Mark 3:29–30.)

The Pharisees had condemned Christ Himself with blasphemy (see John 10:33, 36), and there was His forgiveness for that, but for blasphemy against the Holy Spirit there was no forgiveness, either now or hereafter. Those scribes and Pharisees knew in their hearts that Jesus was virtuous and a true representative of God, yet they declared that He achieved His works by the power of Beelzebub, identifying Jesus with Satan. (See Luke 11:18.) Thus, calling good evil and speaking of evil as being good, they were in grave danger of deadening or killing their conscience. Prejudice and pride can blind men to that which is of God and lead them to attribute the working of the Spirit of God to evil energies and motives.

The unspeakably solemn topic of blasphemy against the Holy Spirit reminds us that if such a sin cannot be forgiven, neither in this world nor in the world to come, how great is our need of forgiveness before we reach this irretrievable state. This particular sin is a state of heart and mind rather than an isolated act. We have the divine assurance that the blood of Jesus Christ is able to cleanse us from all sin, but what is finally unpardonable is the willful, conscious, and final rejection of the pardon God offers man in Christ. There are those who live in fear that they have committed this unpardonable sin, but the very fear they manifest is evidence that they have not committed it, for those who have are insensitive to any fear. Only those who are hardened in heart can attribute a work of mercy and kindness and goodness on the part of Christ to the power of Satan. Fear of committal of this sin against the Holy Spirit is one of the devil's devices to keep despairing hearts from Him who prayed for His murderers, "*Father, forgive them; for they know not what they do"* (Luke 23:34). The solemn task of the teacher is to warn sinners of the peril of procrastination with emphasis upon the old time call *"To day if ye will hear his voice, harden not your hearts"* (Hebrews 4:7).

Jesus summed up His teaching concerning the ministry of the Holy Spirit saying that His death would prepare the way for the coming of the Spirit to His church and that without His death on the cross the gracious work of the Spirit in the church would not be possible. (See John 16:7.) Through all Jesus accomplished by His death, resurrection, and ascension, the gifts and graces are now possible for believers to appropriate. (See Galatians 5:22–23; 1 Corinthians 12:1–11; Ephesians 4:4–13.) The power of the Holy Spirit in our lives today is limited only by the degree of our willingness and capacity to experience the Spirit's fullness. (See Ephesians 5:18.)

Because the teachings of Jesus have a purifying effect and also form a basis of fruitful praying (see John 15:3, 7), how important it is to give heed to His prominent instruction concerning the Holy Spirit. In His reference to the quickening power of the Spirit, *"It is the Spirit that gives life"* (John 6:63 NASB), Jesus went on to affirm that the truths He taught "are Spirit and are life." Godet says that the meaning of the declaration of Jesus is,

> My words are the incarnation and communication of the Spirit;
> it is the Spirit who dwells in them and acts through them; and
> for this reason they communicate life.

COMFORT FROM THE SCRIPTURES

The Bible presents the sublime revelation of the God of all comfort, and was written by holy men directly inspired by the Holy Spirit, the ever-present Comforter, whose mission it is to lead and guide us into all truth. What else could we expect the Bible to be but a well-filled treasury of comforting promises and precepts? Did not the apostle declare that *"things which were written before were written for our learning, that we through the patience and comfort of the scriptures might have hope"* (Romans 15:4 NKJV)? From the very beginning of the recorded word, countless multitudes have found comfort and encouragement in the experiences of Bible characters and in the truths the Spirit enabled them to set forth.

No matter what our calling may be or the trials, sorrows, and disappointments besieging our pathway, there is always a consoling passage to suit our need, to send us on our way rejoicing. To the tired and weary, the Bible is *"the word to him that is weary"* (Isaiah 50:4). To the student, it makes him *"wiser than his teachers"* (Psalm 119:99). To the preacher, it is ever *"in season and out of season"* (2 Timothy 4:2). To the dying, its soothing words *"are spirit, and they are life"* (John 6:63).

> Holy Bible, precious Book
> Into thee I love to look.
> Thou art comfort in distress
> And so many thou canst bless.
> —*Author Unknown*

Whether in times of need, weakness, sickness, poverty, distress, or sin, the Bible has the very message enabling us to manifest *"longsuffering with joyfulness"* and to accept and believe that all things, even the most unwelcome, work together for good, if we are truly the Lord's. (See Colossians 1:11.) The poetess I. S. Stephenson left us the stanza:

> When in sorrow, when in danger, when in loneliness,
> In thy love look down and comfort their distress.

This is what God does, when, in our tribulation, He directs us to some heartening word of His. Solomon makes the bride request, *"Comfort me with apples"* (Song of Solomon 2:5). She wanted to experience the restoring fragrance of this famous fruit and to *be* sustained by its nourishing quality. For the church, which is His bride, the apples can represent His promises and manifold grace to her, the merit of her Husband, the sense of His love, and the fruits of His life, death, and resurrection.

In a truer and fuller way, the tribute of the woman of Tekoah (as she came before the king) may be applied to the Word of God: *"The word of my lord the king shall now be comfortable"* (2 Samuel 14:17). His words are ever soothing and satisfying. When all other comforts flee, He and His Word abide with us.

When saints come to the valley of the shadow of death, they fear no evil, seeing that His rod and staff comfort them. (See Psalm 23:4.) No wonder dear George Herbert of the early sixteenth century could write, "The Book of books, the storehouse and magazine of life and comfort, the Holy Scriptures." The psalmist said, *"Mine eyes fail for thy word, saying, when wilt thou comfort me?"* (Psalm 119:82). We never approach Scripture with such a question in vain. It is through the comfort of the Scriptures hope is born, for it is every the joy and rejoicing of our heart. Through the prophecies and promises we are always comforted. (See 1 Corinthians 14:31; Psalm 119:52.)

COMFORT BY ANGELS

Zechariah gives us a beautiful glimpse of angelic ministry: *"The LORD answered the angel that talked with me with good words and comfortable words"* (Zechariah 1:13). The last five words literally mean *words, consolations*, and the subject of those consolatory words is the love of Jehovah for His people. The promise of her full establishment is predicted by Jeremiah and other prophets. (See Jeremiah 29:10–11.) The mission of angels is a most profitable study. One striking feature of the service of these heavenly visitants is that their appearance to those on earth was generally of a consoling, encouraging nature.

How comforted the frightened shepherds were when they heard an angelic voice announce, *"Fear not: for, behold, I bring you good tidings of great joy, which shall be to all people. For unto you is born this day in the city of David a Saviour, which is Christ the Lord"* (Luke 2:10–11). Surely our desolate world has never received a happier message than this! The angels guarded and consoled Jesus during His fierce contest with the devil. (See Matthew 4:10–11.) During His terrible agony in the garden of Gethsemane, when He sweated, as it were, great drops of blood, *"there appeared an angel unto him from heaven, strengthening him"* (Luke 22:43). This privileged angel fortified Jesus and sustained His sinking nature for the fierce struggle with a cruel foe. How consoled He must have been by the angel's presence and assistance!

COMFORT BY CHRISTIANS

In 1 Corinthians, Paul, without any self-adulation, would exhort the believers in Corinth, *"Be imitators of me, just as I also am of Christ"* (1 Corinthians 11:1 NASB). It has been said that without an original there can be no imitation. Paul's imitation of the Christ he dearly loved and sacrificially served was no artificial, manufactured likeness. Paul was possessed by Him; it was Jesus who reproduced Himself through the life and labors of the apostle. Prominent among the heavenly virtues Paul imitated was that of comfort. He wrote of the *"everlasting consolation"* and *"comfort [for]…hearts"* (2 Thessalonians 2:17), the Lord Jesus gave His own and of the need to comfort others as the outcome of being initially comforted of God. Paul's ministry was conspicuous for its consoling influence, even as it was in the witness of other Bible saints.

Paul also tells the Corinthians that those declaring the oracles of God should do so not only for edification, but for comfort. (See 1 Corinthians 14:3.) The word Paul used here means *kindly, soothingly,* implying persuasive power and great tenderness. When he wrote to the Philippians about consolation in Christ and *"comfort of love"* (Philippians 2:1), he employed a term implying the instrument wherewith the comforter acts, namely, with soothing and consoling words. In his contact with others, he constantly showed this comfort of love. There was nothing cold or perfunctory about his words and acts of comfort. Such comfort may be misunderstood, as was the motivation of David when he sent his servants to comfort Hanun on the death of his father. (See 2 Samuel 10:2.) The leaders treated the agents of comfort as spies and shamefully humiliated them. (See 1 Chronicles 19:1–5.)

Commending his fellow-workers who had comforted him, Paul used a further word for *comfort,* which was the verbal form of a word employed in medicine meaning "to allay irritation." (See Colossians 4:11.) It was in this way the friends he names greatly helped him in his arduous ministry. (See Colossians 4:7–11.)

Paul reveals his heart when he rebukes the carnal Corinthians for their treatment of one who had them in his heart. The care of the church at Corinth was a heavy, irksome load, yet the apostle was *"filled with comfort"* (2 Corinthians 7:4). Beset by fighting and fears within, he could write, *"Nevertheless God, that comforteth those that are cast down, comforteth us by the coming of Titus"* (2 Corinthians 7:6–7), who himself had been greatly consoled by others. (See 1 Thessalonians 3:7.) Then there was Tychicus who, like Paul, was an imitator of the divine Comforter. The apostle sent Tychicus to comfort the hearts of believers in Ephesus and in Colossae. (See Ephesians 6:22; Colossians 4:8.)

Other imitators of the comfort of God mentioned in Scripture are worthy of reference. God Himself was the divine Original, for He said of Israel, His adulterous wife, *"I will allure her, and bring her into the wilderness, and speak comfortably unto her"* (Hosea 2:14). *"Hezekiah spake comfortably unto all the Levites that taught the good knowledge of the LORD"* (2 Chronicles 30:22). Here, the Hebrew word for "comfortably" means "to the hearts of all." When the land was threatened by the invasion of Sennacherib, Hezekiah spake comfortably again to his people, urging them not to be afraid of the arm of flesh, but they were terrified by what would happen if the godless ruler was triumphant. (See 2 Chronicles 32:6–7.) There may be times in our own experience when well-intentioned comfort is spurned.

Job suffered much at the hands of his *"miserable comforters"* (Job 16:2). Still, after his severe trials were over, he was gratified by all his relatives and friends who came and *"comforted him over all the evil that the LORD had brought upon him"* (Job 42:11). They were, indeed, merry comforters. Isaiah was commissioned by the divine Comforter to speak *"comfortably to Jerusalem"* (Isaiah 40:2), which he did with mighty effect, as chapters 40 and 41 of his prophecy reveal.

Sympathetic Jews, learning of the death of Lazarus, hastened to his heartbroken sisters, Mary and Martha, to assure them of their deep sympathy in the family's bereavement. At such a time even the presence of understanding friends is a consolation. (See John 11:19–31.) Think of Barnabas, the Levite, who sold all his land and gave the money to the fast-growing church. He certainly lived up to the meaning of his name, *"the son of consolation"* (Acts 4:36). How the apostles must have been heartened and strengthened by his sacrificial gift!

We live in a desolate, cold, and loveless world. All around us are distressed hearts waiting for a comforter with a human face and sympathetic word to come their way. Are there neighbors who would be greatly cheered by a visit from you? Comforted of God, go out and comfort them which are in any trouble.

> *Praise be to God…who comforts us in all our affliction so that we may be able to comfort those who are in any affliction with the comfort with which we ourselves are comforted by God.*
>
> (2 Corinthians 1:4 NASB)

Did you hear the loving word?
Pass it on!
Like the singing of a bird?
Pass it on!
Let its music live and grow;
Let it cheer another's woe;
You have reaped what others sow—
Pass it on!
—*Author Unknown*

COMFORTED IN DEATH

It might seem macabre to speak of this last enemy awaiting destruction as a consoler. It seems he floods the world with tears. Yet in his poetic tribute to Robert Louis Stevenson, W. E. Henley could write of,

> The friendly and comforting breast
> Of the old nurse, death.

Longfellow, too, in *Evangeline*, has the beautiful couplet:

> And, she looked around, she saw how death, the consoler,
> Laying his hand upon many a heart, had healed it forever.

Could it perhaps have been this sentiment Paul had in mind when he wrote *"to die is gain"* (Philippians 1:21 NIV)? Lazarus, the crippled beggar, full of sores, living on scraps from the rich man's table, had no comforts whatever in this life. There were no comforters to relieve his destitution. Death to him was indeed his consoler, for the angels came and carried him to paradise where he was comforted (see Luke 16:25); but the rich man, who had all the artificial comforters money could buy, did not find death's breath comforting. No angelic consolation was his at the end. Out he went into an eternity of unrelieved torment and remorse for not sharing his good things with a comfortless beggar. In Christ, death to us will indeed be a great consoler, for it will mean not only an absence from a body of sin, but we will find ourselves at home with the Lord. Thus, we can sing in triumph with the apostle,

> *Where, O death, is your victory? Where, O death, is your sting? The sting of death is sin, and the power of sin is the law. But thanks be to God! He gives us the victory through our Lord Jesus Christ.*
> (1 Corinthians 15:55–57 NIV)

> *His dominion is an eternal dominion; his kingdom endures from generation to generation. All the peoples of the earth are regarded as nothing. He does as He pleases with the powers of heaven and the peoples of the earth. No one can hold back his hand or say to him:* "What have you done?"
> (Daniel 4:34–35 NIV)

2

GOD COMFORTS HIS CHILDREN

"I am He who comforts you...I...
covered you with the shadow of my hand."
—Isaiah 51:12, 16 (NIV)

"Your anger has turned away and you have comforted me."
—Isaiah 12:1 (NIV)

What an inspiration it is to magnify God in His sanctuary as the One crowned as "Creator of the rolling spheres ineffably sublime."[1] How uplifting to hear His transcendent attributes of love, mercy, grace, peace, justice, righteousness, and also His omnipotence, omnipresence, and omniscience expounded! But what of His comfort? Is not this, too, a blessed virtue of His which is consistently and continually extolled by Scripture? Then why do we not hear more sermons on this encouraging aspect of His divine nature? Afar off as the God of creation, He is very near to our needy hearts as the God of comfort. No matter what phase of comfort is required, God is able to impart it. Thus, all, meaning the whole of anything, presents God as the Author of comfort, the Source of comfort, and as the One whose presence assures our comfort, a Presence that dispels all gloom, fear, doubt, despair, and discomfort.

Humanity is burdened with sorrow, suffering, sadness, sin, and endless separations. It is in dire need of God who alone is able to comfort *"us in all our tribulation"* (2 Corinthians 1:4). All down the ages,

---

1. Matthew Bridges, "Crown Him with Many Crowns" (1852).

saints have proved that practicing the presence of God is a sure way to experience the comfort of God. Who among us when in distress does not appreciate the physical comforts of home, rest, sleep, and the consolation of kind friends? There is no one, however, who can comfort the inner heart like the One who fashioned it, whoever yearns to ease its load. God alone also knows how to correct and chasten when necessary. Too often we need the rebuke of Eliphaz, who asks, *"Are the consolations of God too small for you?"* (Job 15:11 NASB).

Think for a moment of how the saints of old could praise God for acting as their divine Comforter! David could pray, *"For you, O LORD, have helped me and comforted me"* (Psalm 86:17 NIV).

"May your unfailing love be my comfort, according to your promise to your servant" (Psalm 119:76 NIV). Without doubt, the prophet Isaiah is outstanding as the herald of heaven's consolations. Here are some of his commendations.

> *Comfort, comfort my people, says your God. Speak tenderly to Jerusalem.* (Isaiah 40:1–2 NIV)

> *I, even I, am he who comforts you.* (Isaiah 51:12 NIV)

> *As a mother comforts her child, so will I comfort you.* (Isaiah 66:13 NIV)

Paul also grasped the significance of this warm attribute of God, as his epistles prove. *"May the God who gives endurance and encouragement give you a spirit of unity among yourselves as you follow Christ Jesus"* (Romans 15:5 NIV).

How does the Creator of heaven and earth fulfill the role of the Comforter of bruised hearts? Isaiah uses a most tender figure of speech when he comes to describe the precise nature of divine comfort: *"As one whom his mother comforteth, so will I comfort you"* (Isaiah 66:13). Just how does a mother comfort? Hannah More has the stanza,

> The sober comfort, all the peace which springs
> From the large aggregate of little thing;

> On these small cares of daughter, wife, or friend,
> The almost sacred joys of home depend.

Does not this quality of motherly, sober comfort bind many a home together? In sickness or sorrow any child responds to the affection and compassion of a loving mother. Her kisses, embraces, and smiles soon calm a tiny heart. Although it takes the manifold relationships in which human beings stand to each other to reveal the many-sided character of God, which of a mother as a ministering angel in her home is inexpressibly beautiful and tender. Yet even at her best, a mother is but a pale reflection of the love in the heart of God, as with unfailing tenderness He comforts the weary, wounded spirit of His child.

> The watchful mother tarries nigh
> Though sleep has closed her infant's eye:
> For should he wake and find her gone,
> She knows she could not hear his moan.
> But I am weaker than a child,
> And Thou are more than mother dear;
> Without Thee, heaven were but a wild:
> Without Thee, earth a desert drear.

Isaiah dwells much upon the mother-love of God. It was through him that the message came to God's afflicted people, *"Can a mother forget the baby at her breast and have no compassion on the child she has borne? Though she may forget, I will not forget you! See, I have engraved you on the palms of my hands"* (Isaiah 49:15–16 NIV).

Yet the counterpart of father is also used to emphasize the comforting virtue of God. In seeking to console and encourage his children, a prudent father resorts to rational arguments, rather than to kisses and embraces. David thought of God in this same way. *"As a father has compassion on his children, so the LORD has compassion on those who fear him; for he knows how we are formed, he remembers that we are dust"* (Psalm 103:13–14 NIV). Paul links *"Father of mercies"* and *"God of all comfort"* together in 2 Corinthians 1:3, *"Blessed be the God and Father of our Lord Jesus Christ, the Father of mercies and God of all comfort"* (NASB).

Since God created both male and female, all manly virtues and womanly graces meet in Him. All that is best, holiest, and most gracious in a noble father, and also in a pure-hearted mother, may be found in God, the Source of all holy virtue. He fuses together in His own adorable Person the strong, protective love of the father and the patient, tender, brooding, comforting and sacrificial love of a mother.

So do not be like them; for your Father knows what you need before you ask Him.   (Matthew 6:8 NASB)

Because you are sons, God has sent forth the Spirit of His Son into our hearts, crying, "Abba! Father!"   (Galatians 4:6 NASB)

John Oxenham, in his unique poem, "The Father-Motherhood," combines so fully this double aspect.

> Father and Mother, Thou
> In Thy fully being art—
> Justice with mercy intertwined,
> Judgment exact with love combined,
> Neither complete apart.
> And so we know that when
> Our service is weak and vain,
> The Father—justice would condemn,
> The Mother—love Thy wrath will stem
> And our reprieval gain.

3

COMFORT IN KNOWING
THE WILL OF GOD

Keswick, the name of a beautiful English town, is also a theological expression—a definition of a certain attitude of mind and heart toward God. The term is indicative of a phase of spiritual truth, so dear to the hearts of multitudes of God's people the world over.

Among the exponents of Keswick truth, none was as helpful to me as the late Dr. S. D. Gordon. My first association with him goes back to 1910. While I was a student in Glasgow, Scotland, this renowned Bible expositor visited the well-known Bible Institute there to lecture on John's gospel. His deeply spiritual messages and most unusual style of delivery greatly impressed my formative mind.

After one of Dr. Gordon's remarkable lectures, I ventured to ask him to write something in my autograph album. Kindly obliging, he penned, "The greatest passion that can bum in the human heart is to know the will of God, and get it done." In after years, when it was my joy to become identified as a Keswick speaker, Dr. Gordon and I met again at an annual Manchester Keswick Convention. Rising to give the first message on the opening day, I related the above incident, which gave me the basis of a message on "The Sweet Will of God." Needless to say, Dr.

Gordon was gratified, and during the convention we had many a walk and talk together.

Without doubt, the knowledge and accomplishment of God's will is the greatest passion that can burn in the human heart. The end of life is not to be good, or even to win souls, but to ascertain and achieve the divine will. This should be the chief object of every life.

> *Thy will be done, as in heaven, so in earth.*   (Luke 11:2)

> *Lo, I come…to do thy will, O God.*   (Hebrews 10:7)

How forceful are the words of Theodore Monod, the saintly French theologian, "Ask yonder sun, 'What are you doing?' And he will answer, 'The will of God;' those waves of ocean, and they will answer, 'The will of God;' tiny flower, drinking in the dew, 'What art thou doing?' And it will answer, 'The will of God.' But ask a man, highest of God's creation, 'What are you doing?' and the answer too often is, 'What I choose; I please myself; I do as I will and assert my independence of God as though He were not.'" All around us are those who live as if God were not. His will for their life is of no concern to them. As creatures, they live their lives indifferent to the purpose the Creator had in mind when He fashioned them. They never seem to learn the wisdom so aptly expressed by Tennyson,

> Our wills are ours, we know not why,
> Our wills are ours to make them Thine.

Comparing the physical and spiritual realms, there are parallels one can draw. For example, the first requirement we receive from physical life is food—it is similar in the spiritual life.

> *Jesus saith unto them, My meat is to do the will of him that sent me, and to finish his work.*   (John 4:34)

The next need after food is society, which surrounds us from the hour of our birth. This is also true spiritually.

> *For whosoever shall do the will of my Father which is in heaven, the same is my brother, and sister, and mother.*   (Matthew 12:50)

Then when we reach years of understanding we require a good education, which is so spiritually.

Teach me to do thy will; for thou art my God: thy spirit is good; lead me into the land of uprightness. (Psalm 143:10)

As life develops, we need pleasure in some form or other. The child commences with its toys. Thus is it with the spiritual world.

Above when he said, Sacrifice and offering and burnt offerings and offering for sin thou wouldest not, neither hadst pleasure therein; which are offered by the law. (Hebrews 10:8)

Our whole life, then, can be built upon the vertical column of God's will, and then when life is over,

And the world passeth away, and the lust thereof: but he that doeth the will of God abideth forever. (1 John 2:17)

In this study, we are more concerned with the specific aspect of God's will as it relates to our lives as His professed followers, rather than with His will in connection with the world at large. Phrases are so often found upon our lips like, "If it is His will," or "God willing." It is to be feared, however, that we use these or similar terms all too lightly and without meaning. Then there are times when we confuse our own desires with the will of God. We project our will, confusing it with the divine will, but doubt regarding God's will for every phase of our life will not linger long if we have a sincere desire for all God has for us.

If we yearn to live in the center of God's will as the days go by and as crises arise, there are two preliminary conditions to be faced, namely desire and devotion. Desire amounts to readiness to obey. Devotion must be of a practical nature resulting in the willingness to obey the known will of God at all costs. *"And that servant, which knew his lord's will, and prepared not himself, neither did according to his will, shall be beaten with many stripes"* (Luke 12:47).

Plutarch said of the Grecians, "They knew what was just, but did it not." A man's knowledge can be a torch lighting his way to hell or to heaven. If we know God's will and fail to accomplish it, wherein do we excel hypocrites? How can we call ourselves Christians if we are *knowers* of the divine will, but not *doers* of it? It would be improper to call a man a tradesman if he never wrought at his trade. True Christians are those who know God's will and daily work for its fulfillment.

In his most helpful book, *The Perfect Will of God*, G. Christian Weiss reminds us that once the all-important matter of God's will takes first place in the believer's consciousness, then the whole question of the Christian life takes on a new meaning. "To many this comes as a climatic and revolutionary experience. When once this great truth becomes a *conviction*, the logical result in the heart of every true child of God will be to find out what that will and plan for his life is." As this precious truth becomes a reality, a Christian will get down to serious business seeking "that perfect will of God." There can be little enthusiasm in one's seeking something one is not sure actually exists. Rest assured a divine plan does exist for you. Rest not until you have sought and found that plan for your life.

"The Center of Thy Will"

Safe in the center of Thy loving will,
My God and Father—this indeed is rest!
No sad forebodings now, no dread of ill,
How free from care I am—how truly blest!
Within this place of perfect safety hid,
From henceforth let me evermore abide;
My fears are gone, my restless longing stilled;
My God, I trust Thee and am satisfied.
—*Jane Woodfall*

GOD'S DESIGN FOR EVERY LIFE

Anything man makes is for the service of man. We were fashioned by God's hand for the realization of His will and purpose. Our chief end is to glorify God. We are in the world not as the result of chance or fate, but by divine choice. He made us, and we are His. Of this we can be certain, the Creator never meant any of His creatures to entertain dubiety concerning His will. *"Having made known unto us the mystery of his will, according to his good pleasure which he hath purposed in himself"* (Ephesians 1:9).

While it is true that those who are His redeemed children have to walk by faith, this faith is in One who loves to take His weakest children by the hand and guide them in the way of His will. The Bible produces abundant evidence that God has a plan for every life He made and saved. He never sets a ship to sail over life's tempestuous seas without a rudder. David realized this when he prayed, *"Teach me to do thy will"* (Psalm 143:10). Abraham expressed the same desire.

Paul was ever conscious of God's will for his own life and for the saints of God, his first concern after being saved was to know God's will (Acts 21:14; Romans 12:1–2; Ephesians 5:17; Colossians 1:9; 4:12; Hebrews 10:36). *"And he trembling and astonished said, Lord, what wilt thou have me to do? And the Lord said unto him, Arise, and go into the city, and it shall be told thee what thou must do"* (Acts 9:6).

Peter told the suffering saints, *"It is better, if the will of God be so, that ye suffer for well doing, than for evil doing"* (1 Peter 3:17). John reminded the saints, *"The world passeth away, and the lust thereof: but he that doeth the will of God abideth for ever"* (1 John 2:17). Time and space fail us to enumerate other great examples in the Bible of those who lived in the will of God. Moses, Elijah, Isaiah, and Daniel are among those who came to know God's will and design for their lives, and who were happy in the fulfillment of the divine plan.

The annals of church history are likewise filled with the stories of those who discovered God's will for their lives and who were consumed with an undying passion to realize that will to the full. The story of Betty Stam's radiant life and martyrdom has been beautifully told by Mrs. Howard Taylor in *The Triumph of John and Betty Stam*, both of whom were killed for Christ's sake at Miaosheo. When the call came to Betty to yield her life for service in China, she resisted, saying in her heart to God, "I suppose that you want me to give up all the things that are fun, and to be a stupid old maid missionary, with thick and stubby black shoes and a tight-waisted dress." But Betty's stubborn will was conquered, and she became her Lord's slave.

Writing to her "dearest little sister Bunny" on October 7, 1926, she described how she entered "the only worthwhile way of unconditional surrender to God's will." Mrs. Howard Taylor's own father-in-law, Hudson Taylor, founder of the China Inland Mission, had a similar experience.

To him, to know and accomplish the will of God was a costly matter. He once wrote a moving letter from beside a couch where his beloved daughter lay dying in China. "It was no vain nor unintelligent act," he said, "when, knowing the land, its people and its climate, I laid my wife and children, with myself, on the altar for this service." Surrendering to God's will meant much in sacrifice and hardship to Hudson Taylor, but he did not faint.

The great design of God's will, then, is to make us doers of His will. All of His royal edicts and precepts are for such a purpose. The Word of God is not only a rule of knowledge but of duty. It was written for such an end.

> It is the LORD your God you must follow, and him you must revere. Keep his commands and obey him; serve him and hold fast to him. (Deuteronomy 13:4 NIV)

> The LORD your God commands you this day to follow these decrees and laws; carefully observe them with all your heart and with all your soul. You have declared this day that the LORD is your God and that you will walk in his ways. (Deuteronomy 26:16–17 NIV)

> If you fully obey the LORD your God and carefully follow all his commands I give you today, the LORD your God will set you high above all the nations on earth. (Deuteronomy 28:1 NIV)

> See, I am setting before you today a blessing and a curse—the blessing if you obey the commands of the LORD your God that I am giving you today; the curse if you disobey the commands of the

LORD *your God and turn from the way that I command you today*
by following other gods, which you have not known.

(Deuteronomy 11:26–28 NIV)

The threatenings of God also play their part in the fulfillment of
His will. They stand as an angel with a flaming sword to prevent us
from sinning and to make us doers of His perfect will, *"But God shall*
wound the head of his enemies, and the hairy scalp of such an one as goeth
on still in his trespasses" (Psalm 68:21). The way in which these threatenings laid hold of those who were guilty of disobedience like Saul, serve
to scare us from disobeying the divine will.

Often affliction forces us to an understanding and realization of
God's will in our life. The rod seems to say, "Be ye doers of God's will."
It was so with Manasseh. *"And when he was in affliction, he besought the*
LORD his God, and humbled himself greatly before the God of his fathers"
(2 Chronicles 33:12). Affliction is the furnace in which we are melted
and molded into obedience.

> And Hezekiah prayed…saying,…Incline thine ear, O LORD, and
> hear…the words of Sennacherib, which hath sent to reproach the
> living God. Of a truth, LORD, the kings of Assyria have laid waste
> all the nations…and have cast their gods into the fire: for they were
> no gods, but the work of men's hands, wood and stone: therefore
> they have destroyed them. Now therefore, O Lord, save us from his
> hand. (Isaiah 37:15–20)

Further, the recognition and fulfillment of God's will is our best
certificate of discipleship. We may speak with tongues of angels, but
what avails if we fail to obey God? Doing His will is the best evidence
of our sincerity.

The doing of God's will also furthers the interests of the gospel.
Julian, in one of his *Epistles*, writes to Arsatius, "The Christian religion
did much flourish by the sanctity and obedience of them that professed
it." It is thus with ourselves. Obedience to God's will is the diamond
that sparkles in our witness. The Puritan theologian Thomas Watson
remarked, "Others cannot see what faith is in the heart; but when they

see we do God's will on earth, it makes them have a venerable opinion of religion and become proselytes of it."

Understanding and doing the will of God also proves our love to Him. *"He that hath my commandments, and keepeth them, he it is that loveth me: and he that loveth me shall be loved of my Father, and I will love him, and will manifest myself to him"* (John 14:21).

A child's love for his parents is proven by his gladness and alacrity in obeying their will for his highest interests. We cannot say we truly love God if we slight His commands. Even if His will should cross our own will, our love for our unerring Lord prompts us to obey.

"Though He Slay Me"

Though He slay me, I would rest
In His sovereign will,
For the joy to feel His arms
Wrapped about me still.
Though He slay me, yet in Him
All my soul would trust,
Not, alone, because it may,
But because it must.
—L. A. Bennett

LIFE'S GREAT PROBLEM

How often we hear this expression from others, "My difficulty is how to know what God's will is!" Yet, if they are honest, they will not be long in doubt concerning the precise nature of His will. If they are willing to do God's will, knowledge of it can easily be discerned.

For this cause we also, since the day we heard it, do not cease to pray for you, and to desire that ye might be filled with knowledge of his will in all wisdom and spiritual understanding. (Colossians 1:9)

Dr. F. B. Meyer said our greatest difficulty is simply that we are not willing to be made willing to know and do God's will. *Willing to be made willing!* How true it is that right here is the secret of our spiritual failure! The well-known spiritual guide, James M. McConkey, expressed the same thought in this telling fashion—

> Will to do God's will for your life instead of your own. Do not launch out upon the sea of life headed for a port of your own choosing, guided by a chart of your own draughting, driven by the power of your own selfish pleasures and ambitions. Come to God, yield your life to Him by one act of trustful, irrevocable surrender. ...So shall you come steadily to know and see God's will for your life...without a shadow of a doubt, we will begin to know God's will as soon as we begin to choose His will for our lives instead of our own.

As we approach the scriptural revelation of the divine will, it is imperative to point out that while God has revealed the broad purpose of His will in His Word, He is always ready and willing to unfold His will for our own personal life. He is never reluctant to show us His will. May we be saved from praying and begging as if we had to force God to display His will for our life! Failure to ascertain God's will is always a human failure, never a divine one. God could not be all-loving if He deliberately withheld knowledge of His will from any child of His.

What is meant by God's will? Such a question can quickly be answered. There is His *secret will*, or the will of His decree. Seeing we cannot know His secret will, the same cannot consciously be fulfilled by us. God has secret purposes locked up in His breast, which neither angels nor men possess a key to open. "*It is the glory of God to conceal a thing*" (Proverbs 25:2). Then there is His *revealed will*, which is fully written for us in God's infallible revelation of Himself, namely, the Scriptures. Within such we have the declaration of His will for His church and the world, for time and eternity.

Studying God's will as it is set forth in His Word; we discover it to have many aspects:

Sovereign Will. As the sovereign Lord, He has absolute jurisdiction over us to do with us as He pleases. None can stay His hand saying, "What doest Thou?" He has a supreme right and dominion over those created by His power and redeemed by the blood of His Son. He is not accountable to anyone else for what He does. *"Why dost thou strive against him? for he giveth not account of any of his matters"* (Job 33:13).

None dare summon God to any bar or call Him to account. Who is higher than the Highest? (See Ecclesiastes 5:8.) This sovereign will of God cannot be disputed. As we acknowledge it, submit to it, our discontent is silenced, and all our unruly passions are conquered.

Wise Will. As the God of righteous judgment, we can safely leave Him to judge what is best for us. Therefore we can rest in His wisdom and acquiesce in His will.

> *And therefore will the* LORD *wait, that he may be gracious unto you, and therefore will he be exalted, that he may have mercy upon you: for the* LORD *is a God of judgment: blessed are all they that wait for him.* (Isaiah 30:18)

While traveling over the mighty deep on one of the majestic liners, would we ever think of doubting the skillful pilot? If we questioned his ability to take his ship over the ocean, passengers would rise and protest, "Let him alone; he knows how best to steer is ship." Would that we could realize that God's will is guided by His wisdom! Who else is there to steer our frail barque over life's tempestuous sea? He alone can control the cross-winds of life and bring us to the desired haven. If He does permit us to have our way for a while, it is that we might discover our ignorance. If He leaves us to choose for ourselves, we always choose the worst. Lot chose Sodom because it was well watered and a veritable garden of the Lord. Alas, however, He rained fire upon it out of heaven. (See Genesis 13:9; 19:24.)

Just Will. The will of man, corrupted by sin, is unfit to give law. God's will is a holy, unerring will. God can never do anything wrong. He is never sorry for what He does. *"Shall not the Judge of all the earth do right?"* (Genesis 18:25). God's will is *regula et mensura*, that is, the rule of justice. Lack of wisdom on our part may deem God's will to be unjust, severe, and unkind, but it never is. It is ever a perfect will. As we willingly submit to it, no matter how unjust is appears to be, we come to know how right and beneficial it is. *"Clouds and darkness are round about him; righteousness and judgment are the habitation of his throne"* (Psalm 97:2).

Irresistible Will. Paul asks the question, *"Who hath resisted his will?"* (Romans 9:19). Who has with any measure of success? Man may oppose God's will, but he cannot hinder it. Who can stay the chariot of the sun in its full career? Who can hold back the mighty tides of the ocean? It is vain to contest what God's will determines. Our only attitude is that of submission, "lying low at my Redeemer's feet."

It may be fitting at this point to draw attention to what Dr. C. I. Scofield calls the *directive* and the *permissive* will of God. There is, of course, a great distinction between the two, as we discover in the book of Job, where what God *allows* and what He *sends* are seen to be totally different. While God allowed Satan to afflict His servant Job, He did not send the affliction. The same is true in respect to temptations which God permits but never provides. *"Let no man say when he is tempted, I am tempted of God: for God cannot be tempted with evil, neither tempteth he any man"* (James 1:13).

Scofield expands on this twofold aspect of God's will with a story from Genesis.

> It is important to distinguish between the *directive* and *permissive* will of God. In the first sense the place for the covenant family was Canaan (Genesis 26:1–5). Genesis 46:3 is a touching instance of the permissive will of God. Jacob's family broken, and in part already in Egypt, the tenderness of Jehovah would not forbid the aged patriarch to follow. God will take up His people and, so far as possible, bless them even when they are out of His best. In Israel's choice of a king (1 Samuel 8:7–9); in the turning back from Kadesh (Deuteronomy 1:19–22); in the sending of the spies; in the case of Balaam—illustrations of

this principle are seen. It is needless to say that God's *permissive* will never extend to things morally wrong. The highest blessing is ever found in obedience to His *directive* will.

"The Will Divine"

Thy will, O God, is joy to me, a gladsome thing;
For in it naught but love I see, Whate'er it bring.
I walk by faith, not sense nor sight; Calm faith in Thee;
My peace endures, my way is bright, my heart is free.

4

COMFORT IN GOD'S PROMISES

"When you pass through the waters, I will be with you;
and when you pass through the rivers, they will not sweep over
you. When you walk through the fire, you will not be burned;
the flames will not set you ablaze."
—Isaiah 43:2 (NIV)

The value of a promise depends upon the character of the promiser and his ability to do what he has promised. Thus we know that promises made to us by some people are practically worthless because we are aware of their character. They are untrustworthy; hence, any promise made by them cannot be relied upon. When we come to consider the promises of God, we can at once and without fear, dismiss from our minds any misgivings on any point.

The simple words quoted above from Isaiah should dispel all doubt concerning God's promises, for He cannot lie. (See Titus 1:2.) It is not possible for Him to lie. We may, through ignorance, utter words which are not true, or through failure to recognize our limitations promise what we are unable to carry out. Not so with God. Sometimes He may promise what to man appears an impossible thing, as in the case of Abraham. When God promised Him a son, Abraham was *"fully persuaded that, what he had promised, he was able also to perform"* (Romans 4:21). The faith of Abraham in God's promise was fully justified, as faith in all God's promises is always justified.

I trust His righteous character,
His counsel, promise, and His power;

His honor and His Name's at stake,
To save me from the burning lake.
—*E. Mote*

Every promise, writes Salter, is built upon four pillars: "God's justice or holiness, which will not suffer Him to deceive; His grace or goodness, which will not suffer Him to forget; His truth, which will not suffer Him to change; and His power, which makes Him able to accomplish?"

The promises of God are described by Peter.

His divine power has given us everything we need for life and godliness through our knowledge of him who called us by his own glory and goodness. Through these he has given us his very great and precious promises, so that through them you may participate in the divine nature and escape the corruption in the world caused by evil desires.   (2 Peter 1:3–4 NIV)

There is a promise in God's Word for every possible situation into which the Christian may be brought. A portrait gallery of men and women who trusted in the promises that God made to them can be examined at any time by a reference to Hebrews. One thing, however, that must always be kept in mind is that God's promises are fulfilled in His time and in His way. This often means that we have to wait, and the waiting is not easy for the naturally impatient heart of man desiring to see at once the fulfillment of the promise. The eleventh chapter of Hebrews shows us that in almost every case, these men and women had to wait, as Simeon had to wait "*for the consolation of Israel*" (Luke 2:25). A. L. Waring expresses this aspect beautifully as she sings,

Sometimes I long for promised bliss,
But it will not come too late—
And the songs of patient spirits rise
From the place wherein I wait;
While in the faith that makes no haste
My soul has time to see

A kneeling host of Thy redeemed,
In fellowship with me.

It may be that you have had a promise applied to your heart and are still waiting for its fulfillment. We learn from the Word of God and from the lives of the saints that God often keeps His people waiting, but of this we may be sure: His Word will be fulfilled. He has never failed one who has trusted in Him, whether the promise on which the soul relied related to providence or grace. To take God at His Word is to honor Him.

He has promised grace. He has promised eternal life. He will never break His Word. Happy are those who trust in God's pledged Word at all times, for in trusting thus they will indeed be comforted of God.

Ask and it will be given to you; seek and you will find; knock and the door will be opened to you. For everyone who asks receives; the one who seeks finds; and to the one who knocks, the door will be opened. (Matthew 7:7–8 NIV)

I have enjoyed many of the comforts of life, none of which
I wish to esteem lightly; yet I confess I know not any joy that
is so dear to me, that so fully satisfies the inmost desires of my
mind, that so enlivens, refines, and elevates my whole nature,
as that which I derive from religion—from faith in God.
May this God be thy God, thy Refuge, thy Comfort,
as He has been mine.
—*Lavater*

5

COMFORT WHEN GOD
SEEMS ABSENT

"Truly you are a God who hides himself."
—Isaiah 45:15 (NIV)

"Jesus left that place and went to the vicinity of Tyre.
He entered a house and did not want anyone to know it;
yet he could not keep his presence secret."
—Mark 7:24 (NIV)

The two phrases introducing this phase of heavenly comfort are complementary. No man has seen God at any time, and in this sense God hides Himself from our view. In Jesus, His beloved Son, however, we have a perfect and final revelation of the Father, which constrained Christ to confess, *"He that hath seen me hath seen the Father"* (John 14:9). While Jesus lived among men, He could not be hid.

Isaiah's strange words apparently charge the Lord with being negligent of His people while they were in exile and bondage. Either He had forgotten them, or they had forgotten Him. With clearer light, however, they came to trace His footprints. God had appeared to be unseen, indifferent, but now the people discovered He had ever been at work on their behalf, overruling all things for His glory and for their good. Compare the lines below from an unknown poet with the message of Isaiah.

He hides Himself so wondrously
As if there were no God.
He is least seen when all the powers
Of ill are most abroad.

The verse is one of those passages which bristles with great thoughts. What honey there is in this piece of rock! In how many ways does God in love and providence delight to hide Himself!

GOD IS HIDDEN

In His Being. Paul tells us that God *"is the King eternal, immortal, invisible"* (1 Timothy 1:17 NIV); and, again, that He is *"who only hath immortality, dwelling in the light which no man can approach unto; whom no man hath seen, nor can see"* (1 Timothy 6:16).

No human being has ever witnessed God's divine essence. He dwells in glory inaccessible, hiding Himself from the gaze of inferior beings. A faint idea of its dazzling fullness may be gathered from the transfiguration of our Lord, when the disciples were partially blinded by the effulgence of His inherent glory.

John declared *"no man hath seen God at any time"* (John 1:18). No one could see Him and live. John himself fell as dead at the feet of the glorified Lord. Moses came nearest to seeing God.

> *Then Moses said, "Now show me your glory." And the* LORD *said, "I will cause all my goodness to pass in front of you, and I will proclaim my name, the* LORD, *in your presence. I will have mercy on whom I will have mercy, and I will have compassion on whom I will have compassion. But," he said, "you cannot see my face, for no one may see me and live." Then the* LORD *said, "There is a place near me where you may stand on a rock. When my glory passes by, I will put you in a cleft in the rock and cover you with my hand until I have passed by. Then I will remove my hand and you will see my back; but my face must not be seen."*   (Exodus 33:18–23 NIV)

Even the seraphim veil their faces in His august presence. Before the blinding glory of His radiant holiness, with two of their wings they cover themselves.

> From image of the Infinite
> Whose essence is concealed
> Brightness of uncreated light
> The heart of God revealed.
> —*Author Unknown*

In His Creation. What a hiding of His power there is in the natural real. (See Habakkuk 3:4.) Truly, it is the glory of God to conceal things. (See Proverbs 25:2.) The great discoveries of men in the world of science are but the unfolding of what God originally hid in nature! Gold, silver, coal, precious gems, uranium, and other treasures were deposited in the earth and left there for man to find. All the remarkable inventions of recent years like radar, television, and so on, are simply the harnessing of forces which God placed in the world when He fashioned it. When Kepler made his fascinating discovery of the stellar heavens, he declared that he was only "thinking God's thought after Him." Obadiah has the suggestive word, *"How are his hidden things sought up!"* (Obadiah 1:6). This is what man is doing in his laboratory discoveries; he is searching out what God has hidden. Thus Solomon was right when he wrote, *"There is no new thing under the sun"* (Ecclesiastes 1:9). What are to us amazing discoveries were known ages ago when the Creator wrapped them up in creation. This truth is likewise evident that God has allowed hidden things to be discovered in successive stages. As need has arisen, man has been permitted to unlock the natural treasures to meet it.

In His Book. What did David mean when he prayed, *"Hide not thy commandments from me"* (Psalm 119:19)? Was it not that God sometimes hides behind the lattice of truth? He shows Himself, but it is from behind a curtain. David did not want the Lord to keep from him the inner sense or meaning of His Word. It is only the Spirit-taught who can trace Him.

Of course prejudice, disobedience, and sin can keep God hidden from one's gaze as the Scriptures are read: *"They understood not this saying, and it was hid from them"* (Luke 9:45). Revelation, however, comes with obedience: *"I have showed thee new things from this time, even hidden things"* (Isaiah 48:6).

Often we come to God's holy Book and see nothing out of the ordinary. At other times we rejoice over what we discover as one who finds great spoil. Yet the truth was there all the time. When we depend upon the Holy Spirit, who inspired the Word, a glory gilds the sacred page. Our eyes are opened to behold wondrous things out of God's law. As we read, our contact with the sanctifying truth changes our beliefs, our loves, and our habits. Quietly, unseen by others and even unobserved by ourselves, the Word becomes flesh and dwells among us.

GOD IS REVEALED

In His Providence. There are times in our lives when, amid adverse circumstances, it does seem as if Isaiah's word about God hiding Himself is true. He appears either to have departed or to have veiled His face from the eye of faith.

Take some of life's mysterious aspects. The testimony of Bible saints is that sometimes God conceals Himself in the day of trouble (Psalm 10:1; 44:24; Job 13:24). When Mary and Martha sent for Jesus to come and heal their sick brother Lazarus, Jesus delayed and hid Himself for several days. At Calvary, the Father's face was hidden from the Savior Himself.

How true it is that there are many hidden things which no human skill can unravel! We have to walk in the dark with God. Dr. Moffat translates one basic text, "Yours is indeed the God of mystery, a God that saves." At times the heart of man is mystified by the providential dealings of heaven. God veils the purposes of what He permits, and we see through a glass darkly.

Or take the problem of unanswered prayer. The psalmist pleads with God not to turn His face away as if resolved not to listen to his cry, *"Give ear to my prayer, O God; and hide not thyself from my supplication"* (Psalm 55:1). There are seasons when we pray for necessary, legitimate things, but the heavens appear to be closed and no answer is received.

The one who hears and answers the prayers of others apparently turns and hides Himself from our needs. Adversity, failure, and disappointments sometimes seem to indicate God has forgotten to be gracious.

In one's life there may be a radical cause for His hiding. If the life is displeasing to the Lord, then the smile of His face can never be expected. *"When you hide your face, they are terrified; when you take away their breath, they die and return to the dust"* (Psalm 104:29 NIV). The lack of divine favor should ever give us troubled hearts. Jesus hid Himself from those who failed to love and obey him. (See John 12:36.) Oh, may the benediction of His countenance be our abiding portion! May we never consciously indulge in anything that would cause Him to hide from our vision!

In His Son. Isaiah's cryptic word may likewise be applied to Christ, God's Son, our Savior. The Father hid Himself in His beloved Son, for God was in Christ reconciling the world unto Himself. The most wonderful veiling of the Almighty is associated with Jesus, who alone gazed upon the father. *"No man can see Me and live!"* was God's pronouncement through Moses (Exodus 33:20 NASB). It is only as we see God in Christ that we can live, presently and eternally. *"No man hath seen God at any time, the only begotten Son, which is in the bosom of the Father, he hath declared him"* (John 1:18). Again, *"He that hath seen me hath seen the Father"* (John 14:9). Often in the Old Testament, God veiled Himself in angelic form or appeared as a man. In the Gospels He was incarnate in Jesus; "Veiled in flesh the Godhead see" (Wesley 1734).

In this dispensation God moves in His silent, hidden, mysterious way upon the hearts of men through the ministry of His unseen Spirit. *"The wind blows wherever it pleases. You hear its sound, but you cannot tell where it comes from or where it is going. So it is with everyone born of the Spirit"* (John 3:8 NIV). This is the Comforter to whom Jesus bequeathed His own.

In His People. Again the prophet's words can be made to imply the deeper mystery of the hiding of God within one's own being. The world cannot see the Father, Son, and Holy Spirit, yet all three are buried in our lives. Every believer is a mysterious cabinet of the Trinity. The mystical truth hid from the past ages but taught by the apostle Paul concerns the indwelling Christ: *"Christ in you, the hope of glory"* (Colossians 1:27 NIV). Oh, for a fuller realization of this sublime truth!

When Jesus was here among men, *"He could not be hid"* (Mark 7:24). It was quickly "noised" abroad when he entered a house. (See Mark 7:24; 2:1.) Who can hide the fragrance of a rose, the glory of a sunset, the heat of a fire? If we live in unbroken communion with the three holy Persons residing within our hearts, They are bound to express Their hidden Selves. The aroma and power of this presence will soon be detected by those around who are swift to discern the charm of a God-possessed life. Then may we pray,

O God, hide Thyself deep in my being,
And through my life, so natural yet divine,
Reveal Thyself to a world of sin!

"I learned that it is possible for us to create light and sound and order within us, no matter what calamity may befall us in the outer world."
—*Helen Keller*

PART II

COMFORT IN
THE CHANGES OF LIFE

6

GOD'S PURPOSE FOR CHANGE

"God...will hear them and afflict them—men who never change
their ways and have no fear of God"
—Psalm 55:19 (NIV)

"I the Lord do not change."
—Malachi 3:6 (NIV)

David's career was certainly not a monotonous one. Such drastic events were crowded into it. No wonder he could write, *"Men who never change their ways and have no fear of God"* (Psalm 55:19). No changes! Of whom can it be said, "He has a life without change"? Any person without change must be especially fortunate. "Change and decay in all around I see."

The world is the scene of perpetual change. The sun rises and sets, the moon waxes and wanes, the tides rise and fall. Seed-time and harvest, summer and winter, day and night, come and go. While we cannot take the psalmist's declaration in a literal sense, changes come alike to all, even the inevitable change to which Job refers, *"All the days of my appointed time will I wait, till my change come"* (Job 14:14).

The changes of which David speaks are those changes we least expect, changes that disturb, unhinge our plans and arrangements, and frustrate our hopes. Changes like earthquakes upheave all order, comfort, and settled ease. Without such changes we are liable to drift into

the perils of an undisturbed life, and pleasant monotony breeds ignorance of God. When a man's life is filled with blessings and is never
darkened by storms, there is the fear that the absence of change will rob
him of deeper holiness of life.

David, as we have already hinted, was a man of many conditions.
He was much tried yet much favored. The circumstances of the psalm
from which our text is taken refer to the tragic era in the psalmist's
life when he found himself betrayed by his trusted counselors, and his
confidence was well-near shaken. But his trials finally drove him nearer
God. He knew only too well that uninterrupted prosperity was apt to
cause neglect of higher things.

When a train of troubles attends us and we look at our afflictions,
losses, and crosses, and cry out, "All these changes are against me!" let us
take comfort in reading the history of David and listen to his acknowl-
edgment, *"It is good for me that I have been afflicted"* (Psalm 119:71). God
is always concerned about our highest good, and He gives us medicine
as well as pleasant food.

We know there are those who devise plans and always succeed. All
vessels they launch have prosperous voyages and return heavily laden
with rich cargo. In some cases these men of affluence are not very religious. Worldly in life and not too particular about morality and hon-
esty, they yet succeed where godly men fail.

"I said in my prosperity, 'I will never be moved'" (Psalm 30:6 NASB).
The prosperity of the placid life often produces self-confidence and
forgetfulness of God. When the heart has all it wishes for and freedom from impoverishing changes, the need for God is not very acute.
Unbroken prosperity is spiritually dangerous. One who does nothing
but win and prosper is seldom a chastened, spiritually refined, sympathetic person. Uninterrupted, monotonous success sometimes breeds
atheism.

The paradox of faith, however, is that we are built up by being
broken down. God does by undoing; He makes as He breaks. Reverses
and changes are tools for the shaping of character. Change is a phase of

divine ministry. God takes us back to move us forward. The waves go out and return with fuller force.

There are others whose life is in another direction, like a placid lake. To them health is wealth. A body without sickness or pain is greater riches than silver by far. Such a priceless boon can become just as much a peril as material wealth. Perfectly healthy men are apt to forget they are only a house of clay, so energy is dissipated. The march of life is taken with the step and eye of a giant. No restraint is experienced. Weariness, pain, and despondency never impede progress. Further, the enjoyment of uniformity in the matter of physical blessings often creates indifference to the evident need of those who suffer. Compassion is dried up. Pain in stricken lives is not understood.

Others seem to have unbroken successes, a life without change. Their circle of social life is wonderfully free of the ordinary calamities. God holds back desolating grief, yet He is never thanked. The even tenor of their lives does not bring repentance. A sheltered life is taken as a matter of course; no songs rise to Him from whose hand come all good things. Yet stagnant waters become putrid. Summer heat breeds obnoxious insects. To be without trouble can mean that one is without God. Immunity has its perils.

Life's changes always should and constantly do awaken fear and lead us nearer to God. They are stepping stones to marvelous experiences. What are some of the lessons we learn from our many upheavals? There is, first of all, the sovereignty of God. Amid all the troubles of life, one increasing purpose runs. All the varied threads are in the hands of the perfect Weaver.

Severe changes overtake us, life is emptied of treasures, hopes and ambitions are blasted, and the first reaction of our agony is to think God is cruel. With calmer reflection we withdraw our hard feelings and tell Him He does all things well.

Then there is the unchangeableness of God. David knew that amid all his changes. God was unchanging in His character, purpose, and love. He is without change. Dr. Joseph Parker has it, "If He were always performing some conjuring trick on the battlements of heaven, the attention of the universe might be called to Him." Because of a certain sameness in God, men do not fear Him as they should.

We have difficulty taking our days separately. We must learn, however, to put all our days together and not to look at one day crowned with success and another shadowed with trial and failure. Sublime victory is ours when we realize that all our days, with all their changes, have resulted in our likeness to the unchangeable One.

Perhaps David's message regarding the perils of the changeless life has never really gripped us. Are there perils to fear? Yes, there are dangers, but may we be spared them!

One of the greatest blessings of life is a tender heart. To be without love for God or man is indeed tragic. A person is practically useless in respect to service in a world of need if lacking sympathy. No one can understand the sorrows of others if no trials have been experienced.

Why, if life were made up of no other class than those who have no changes and who, consequently, are past feeling, the world would be a cold place in which to live! Thank God it is otherwise! Amid the anguish of the world there are those who, because they served in the school of grief and were refined in the crucible of change, are able to exercise the ministry of comfort. There are no hands as gentle as those that have known affliction. Jesus is able to come to the aid of tempted souls, seeing he was tempted in all points like as we are, yet without sin.

A life without change is apt to make one materialistic. Materialistic people have their portion in this life, and they live for it as well as in it. Any thought of the future is unwelcome. Their state is a happy, uninterrupted one. Circumstances for them are never altered or disturbed, and consequently their affections are set on earthly things. There is no desire to see God. Because the sufferings of this present world have not come their way, there is little desire for heaven.

Where do we stand in all this? What view of life is ours? Do we look at it as something by and for itself? Do we only live for present enjoyments, scorning the disturbing and unwelcome changes reaching others? Do we put earthly and personal comforts in the place of the divine Comforter? If so, He will put such comforts out of our reach that He alone might become our comfort in life and death.

Are we blind to the fact that the disruptions we despise can make for the ennoblement of character that we can climb to God by this path of pain? If this is the way we look at life, then we are not among the victorious army that blesses the world. If, on the other hand, we have learned to make changes minister unto us, if loss has yielded gain, if poverty has produced wealth, then ours is life indeed. We live on the victory side when we know all our changes only serve to remind us that we have no continuing city in this world of change. When some sorrow plunges deep into heart and home, is it not consoling and blessed to believe that amid all life's drastic changes, the God who changes not is ever near to cause all things to work together for our good?

> Lord, make me an instrument of your peace.
> Where there is hatred, let me sow love,
> Where there is injury, pardon;
> Where there is doubt, faith;
> Where there is despair, hope;
> Where there is darkness, light;
> Where there is sadness, joy.
> O divine Master, grant that I may not so much seek
> To be consoled, as to console,
> To be understood, as to understand,
> To be loved, as to love,
> For it is in giving that we receive;
> It is in pardoning that we are pardoned;
> It is in dying that we are born to eternal life.
> —*Francis of Assisi*

7

COMFORT IN TIMES OF TEMPTATION

"I am my beloved's, and his desire is toward me."
—Song of Solomon 7:10

"Satan hath desired to have you."
—Luke 22:31

One aspect of our consolation in Christ is that He knew what it was to be tempted of the Devil. One impressive feature of His temptation is His willingness to be assailed by the Devil that He might be able to help (succor) those tempted by such an adversary. (See Hebrews 2:18.) The word used here for succor means to run at the cry for help or to advance in aid for one in need. Is it not comforting and encouraging to know that when we are sorely tried by the enemy, Jesus hears our cry for help and hastens to our deliverance?

When temptations gather,
Breathe that Holy Name in prayer.

Second, although Jesus was tempted in all points like we are, He emerged from every contest victorious, or apart from sin. (See Hebrews 4:15.) There is no sin in being tempted. The sin comes in yielding to temptation.

Yield not to temptation,
For yielding is sin.

Had Jesus yielded at any point, He would not have been the sinless Savior. He would likewise have forfeited the authority and power to advance in aid when tempted ones look to Him for victory.

We often fail to realize what a ceaseless conflict rages between the Savior and Satan for the mastery of the soul, as the two verses in the beginning of this chapter indicate. These passages express the deep, solemn truth concerning rival bidders for the souls of man. One bidder is heavenly, the other hellish; one sacred, the other satanic; one fair, the other foul; one beautiful, the other bestial; one blesses, the other blasts; one is the reigning Lord, the other a raging lion.

The conflict for the mastery of a human life greatly resembles an auction room with its atmosphere of eagerness among bidders to secure the priceless goods offered. No two bidders can secure the same article since it is to be "knocked down" to the highest bidder. With such a figure, then, before our minds, let us apply it to the battle for the possession of precious souls, souls that Christ desires in fullness, souls whom the enemy would threaten at any chance.

We have, first of all, the auction room, which is the inner life, the hidden chambers of the heart. Then come the rival bidders, the Savior and Satan, the Lord and the liar. The treasures for auction are the possessions of one's whole being. The auctioneer, who disposes of his wares, we may identify as the will of man, the deciding factor in matters relating to the soul.

THE AUCTION ROOM

The auction room is both seen and unseen. It may also be your study as you ponder this chapter or a church as you listen to the gospel being preached. When you enter God's house, great issues confront you. Rivals are there, earnestly desiring to have you. Holy voices urge you to repent; hellish influences encourage you to reject the Savior.

The auction room is also your own heart. Man's innermost being is ever the ultimate battlefield. The Savior with eyes of love, a heart of compassion, and hands of mercy stands before the soul. With the wooing notes of grace, He strikes to win the allegiance He truly deserves. Satan, with his devilish hatred, his diabolical purpose, and his hands stained with the blood of multitudes both in and out of hell, likewise waits to clutch the sinner, who, understanding the claims of these rival bidders, must knock down his soul to one of them.

THE RIVAL BIDDERS

The initial verses have a direct application to the Christian, for within the Christian there is the constant struggle for mastery. Satan, of course, realizes that he cannot repossess a saved person, but he knows he can cripple the testimony of a Christian. The enemy desired to have Job. *"My desire is that Job may be tried unto the end"* (Job 34:36). Until our end, Christ and Satan will be ever in conflict over the mastery of our life. The Devil will take advantage of God's permission to tempt us. By subtle devices he will try to wreck our witness and send us maimed to heaven. It was thus that he desired to have Peter. (See Luke 22:31.) There the word desire means to ask exclusively for or to practically demand. Christ's intercession on Peter's behalf prevailed, however, over the enemy's purpose.

Let us make no mistake about the fact that Satan desires to have the saints—that is, to ruin their spirituality or to keep them from realizing the fullness of the blessing of God. Christ, on the other hand, yearns for the believer's sanctification. As the King of saints, He greatly desires their beauty. (See Psalm 45:11.) Before the kinsman will hand over such a treasure to one of them, he must know the characters of the rival bidders for his soul.

Who is Satan? How does the Bible describe him? He is the Serpent, subtle and cunning in his approach. He is the adversary, the antagonist of God and man. He is the Devil, a name meaning to throw down. He is a murderer and is responsible for wars, murders, and suicides. He is a liar, a deceiver. Falsity is his chief stock in trade. The prince of demons, he marshals all evil forces for your destruction. He is the roaring lion, devouring, savage, out to consume. He is Apollyon, a destroyer of all that is good and fair. He is the Dragon, bestial, hateful, and fierce. He is an angel of light, plausible, gilding his hollow pleasures. How can man be content to follow and serve this hound of hell? He has no good intentions toward any soul!

Who is the Savior? He is the one who created us all, and Who loves us with an undying love. He is the Beloved, the Shepherd, and the Friend. He is the fairest among ten thousand. His name is an ointment poured forth. He is the Way, the Truth, and the Life. He was the Lamb dying for the sin of the world. Can it be that you see no beauty in Him? Does He have no form or comeliness for you? Blinded by sin and prejudice, do you see Him only as a root out of a dry ground? Does His name not thrill your soul? Has His Word no charm for you?

Consider, in the next place, the contrast of their histories! What is the record of Satan? It is as black as his character! He is who created sorrow among the angels, who was responsible for the entrance of sin, the murder of Abel, the desolation of the flood, and for the tears, graves, sins, sobs, and miseries of mankind all down the ages. The darkness and terrible sins of heathenism, the appalling, iniquitous practices all around, the cesspool of evil within the heart of man are alike the product of Satan's wicked mind. Yet, when this fiend presses his claims, multitudes hand over the precious possession of life without a thought. What a folly!

Has the Savior a different testimony? Can we safely trust our souls to His care? Scripture reveals Him as the obedient One, loving and loved by all who appreciate His worth. (See Proverbs 8:30–31.) As the Creator and Sustainer of everything that lives, He bountifully supplies all necessary meat in due season. Condescending, sympathizing, suffering was He as He lived among men; His passion to save men led Him to be crucified in cold blood. He ever yearned over souls that life eternal might be theirs. He never thought a wrong thought, uttered a wrong word, or committed a wrong action. None could convince Him of sin. He was holy, harmless, undefiled, separate from sinners, higher than the highest, better than the best. Oh, what a Savior! And yet so many treat Him with contempt and slam the door of their hearts in the face of this best Friend.

What motives activate these bidders as they strive for the supremacy over the hearts of men? Is there any conflict in their respective desires?

Take Satan! Is he inspired by good intentions as he approaches man? Good intentions! Why, he is just as much a stranger to those as he is to the truth! He is out for the delusion of the soul, for its loss now and its damnation hereafter. His heart is filled with a diabolical purpose to blast souls and to keep them in the lake of fire eternally. Knowing that he himself is without hope, he labors incessantly to send people to hell with the Christ-less. Ever before him is the destruction of the work of the Trinity on behalf of a sinning world.

Take Jesus! What are His thoughts toward us as He stands and pleads, "*Come unto me*" (Matthew 11:28)? Are they thoughts of peace, as He urges us to join Him in His chariot? Well, His desire to help us can be proved by the fact that He was revealed to destroy the works of the Devil for all sinning souls. Now, untiringly, He labors to deliver men from the penalty and tyranny of sin. He seeks the ennoblement of life and the enrichment of it by the impartation of His own fragrant life. He offers weary hearts present rest and eternal bliss. Our good is ever His wish. But can you understand it? There are many who are yet content to feed on ashes or the husks the swine eat rather than on the bread of the Father's house. Thrice happy are the souls who can say, "O Christ, Thou are my supreme joy! Thy blessed will and mine are one. I have no desires but Thine, no pleasures but such as please Thy holy heart?'

THE TREASURES FOR AUCTION

What are the goods exposed for sale? Are the lots for disposal rare and costly? The truth is that no auctioneer's catalog ever contained such valuable treasures, for did not Jesus declare that one soul is worth more than all the world contains?

The treasures for auction, then, are the whole being, time, talents, possessions, influence, and eternal destiny of a soul. All that we are and have must go to one bidder or the other. Both Christ and Satan appraise the worth of a soul, and they struggle in different ways for its possession.

To lose one's wealth is much.
To lose one's health is more.
To lose one's soul is such a loss
That nothing can restore.
—*Gospel Herald*

What wisdom we show when we permit the Savior to save the soul and have it in His eternal care!

THE AUCTIONEER

With such costly possessions before the bidders, surely the auctioneer must be weighted down with the sense of responsibility as to their right disposal. Pearls of greatest price must not be thrown away for a mere pittance. Who, then, is the auctioneer? Your will is the auctioneer, for upon the human will rests the solemn responsibility as to who shall have the soul. The will listens to the bids and then makes the choice. When Christ and Barabbas were on his hands, Pilate cried, "*Whether of the twain will ye that I release unto you?*" (Matthew 27:21). Your will is your Pilate making a choice between Christ and Satan. Pilate, we read, "*Released unto them him...whom they desired*" (Luke 23:25). The fatal choice that day was Barabbas. On the other hand, we have the record of those who desired to see Jesus. (See John 12:21.) Some desired Barabbas! Others desired Jesus! Who has your allegiance? Can you truthfully confess, "*Whom have I in heaven but thee? and there is none upon earth that I desire beside thee*" (Psalm 73:25)? Your will is ever the deciding factor as to the one to be the master of your life.

During an open-air service, Rowland Hill watched as a woman rode by in her horse and coach while he preached. When he glanced at her, he noticed she was bedecked with jewels and seemed quite self-satisfied as she nestled in the corner of her coach. The truth she heard from earnest lips that day has been cast in the following form.

"The Three Bidders"

Will you listen, friends, for a moment while a story I unfold:
A marvelous tale, of a wonderful sale of a noble lady of old;

How hand and heart at an auction mart, soul and body she
was sold.

And now in His name a sale I proclaim,
And bids for this fair lady call.
Who will purchase the whole—her body and soul, Coronet,
jewels and all?

I see already three bidders—
The world steps up as the first.
I will give her treasures, and all the pleasures
For which my votaries thirst.
She shall dance each day, more joyous and gay
With a quiet grave at the worst.

But out speaks the devil boldly:
The kingdoms of earth are mine,
Fair lady, thy name with an envied fame
On their brightest tablets shall shine.
Only give me thy soul and I give thee the whole,
Their glory and wealth to be thine.

And pray, what hast Thou to offer,
Thou Man of Sorrows unknown?
And He gently said, "My blood I have shed,
To purchase her for mine own.
To conquer the grave, and her soul to save
I trod the winepress alone.
I will give her my cross of suffering,
My cup of sorrow to share,
But with endless love, in my home above,
All shall be righted there.
She shall walk in the light, in a robe of white,
And a radiant crown shall wear.

Thou hast heard the terms, fair lady,
That each hath offered for thee.
Which wilt thou choose, and which will thou lose
This life, or the life to be?
The fable was mine, but the choice is thine,
Sweet lady, which of the three?"

She took from her hands the jewels,
The coronet from her brow.
"Lord Jesus," she said, as she bowed her head,
"The highest bidder art Thou.
Thou gav'st for my sake Thy life, and I take
Thy offer—and take it now.
I know the world and her pleasures
At best they weary and cloy;
And the Tempter is bold, but his houses and gold
Prove ever a fatal decoy.
I long for Thy rest—Thy bid is the best, Lord, I accept it with
joy?"
—*Rowland Hill*

Believing, then, that Christ's bid is the best, may we ever receive it with the consolation the comforting Sprit can impart.

8

COMFORT WHEN SAINTS SIN

"If we say we have no sin, we deceive ourselves."
—1 John 1:8

"I am thine, save me."
—Psalm 119:94

"My dear children, I write this to you so that you will not sin.
But if anybody does sin, we have tone who speaks to the Father in
our defense—Jesus Christ, the Righteous One.
He is the atoning sacrifice for our sins, and not only for ours but
also for the sins of the whole world."
—1 John 2:1–2 (NIV)

The angel of the Lord, in announcing the birth of the Savior, declared that His name should be Jesus because His would be the power to save His people from their sins. The deep significance of such a gracious message is sometimes missed as we give it a too general application; although, of course, it is perfectly legitimate to do so. We must not use it exclusively to describe the great work of salvation in the lives of those who realize their sinfulness.

Note the precise language of this angelic utterance, *"He shall save his people from their sins"* (Matthew 1:21). Such a declaration implies that Jesus is a Savior for saints as well as for sinners, that there is a gospel for the redeemed and regenerated, as well as for the rebellious. So we come to the theme under consideration, namely, the salvation of which we as Christians stand in deep need.

THE SAVIOR FOR SINNERS

Paul gives us the gospel for a world of lost sinners in the words, *"Christ Jesus came into the world to save sinners"* (1 Timothy 1:15). Such a message proclaims Him to be the Savior of mankind, irrespective of race, position, or condition. Let me stop a moment to ask you if, as a lost sinner, have received Christ as your personal Savior? If not, then, here and now, you can prove Him to be the Savior, mighty to save, and strong to deliver.

THE SAVIOR OF HIS PEOPLE

"Thou shalt call his name Jesus: for he shall save his people from their sins" (Matthew 1:21). Here, *"his people"* were those in covenant relationship with Him, namely, the Jews. Of course, there is a sense in which we are all His people, seeing that all of us were brought into being by His divine, creative art. In Matthew 1:21, it is those beyond this connection who are implied. The message is to those who are already His, *"I am thine, save me"* (Psalm 119:94). What a comforting truth!

Further, the word used is *"sins,"* not *sin*. The Lord Jesus is the Savior of saints in that He seeks to save them from the fruit as well as from the root of sin. When we receive Him as our Savior in response to the appeal of the gospel, He deals with the principle of sinning which is ours from birth. The appropriation of the finished work of the Cross means we are made the recipients of a new life. The inner meaning of the verse implies that we are following on to know the power of Christ more completely in heart and life. It means deliverance from the fruit of sin, that is, from the different manifestations of the evil principle or inbred sin. The root was dealt with at the cross, but the fruit remains. Thus Jesus is *"the Savior of all men, and especially of those who believe"* (1 Timothy 4:10 NIV). The first aspect of salvation is dependent upon the death of Christ. He died for sin and rose again to justify the sinner. As we receive Him by faith, we are saved from the penalty and guilt of sin. The second aspect, however, is dependent upon His intercession. We are saved by His life, not the example of His spotless, earthly life, but by His present, risen, glorified life. (See Romans 5:10.) *"He is able also to save them to the uttermost that come unto God by him, seeing he ever liveth to make intercession for them"* (Hebrews 7:25).

SINS FROM WHICH THE LORD DESIRES TO SAVE HIS PEOPLE

We now come to deal with some of the sins from which the Lord desires to save His people. In doing so, let us look at those apart from the sins grossly sinful and manifestly evil. It is taken for granted that we are not engaging in any known sin.

> *Nevertheless, God's solid foundation stands firm, sealed with this inscription: "The Lord knows those who are His," and, "Everyone who confesses the name of the Lord must turn away from wickedness."*　　　　　　　　　　(2 Timothy 2:19)

If any of us have the slightest secret sympathy with some hidden sin, may God in His mercy expose it and save us! Here, then, are a few of the sins of saints.

The Bitterness of Criticism. Bitter, unworthy, and unChristlike criticism is the dead fly causing the ointment of many a good life to send forth a stinking savor. Miriam, the prophetess, was severely punished by God for her harsh criticism of Moses, the leader of the Israelites. Whether you are in a church or some other group, believe in it and serve it with your utmost loyalty. Yes, and shield the faulty ones in the flock, not exposing one's dirty linen to public gaze. If you do not altogether agree with a preacher, be silent about your critiques before the godless. Do not tear your preacher or any of your fellow church members to pieces before children. To be guilty of dragging the failure of a church, preacher, or Christian before the world is to act as a traitor in the camp. This is a sin of which we are all more or less guilty. We may count ourselves separated and sanctified in that we never smoke, drink, or go to places of worldly amusement and yet be known as wretched gossipers and backbiters.

The Burden of Discontent. One of the outstanding sins of God's people, the Jews, under the old economy, was discontent. *"When the people complained, it displeased the LORD"* (Numbers 11:1). They grumbled, murmured, and complained until God had to punish them. Now a discontented Christian is a contradiction of the Savior we profess to serve, seeing He has told us to *"be content"* (Luke 3:14). Paul tells us that *"godliness with contentment is great gain"* (1 Timothy 6:6 NIV). Both should go together, although, alas, these twin sisters are sometimes parted. Here are some ways discontentment operates.

We are discontented with our circumstances. Our sphere becomes monotonous. We are not happy with the people around us. Things worry and annoy us, eating into our souls like canker. We feel we should be better off than we are, should have a higher position or a more lucrative one. Oh, how we have to give heed to the injunction, *"Be content with such things as ye have"* (Hebrews 13:5).

We are discontented with the weather. The weather causes more grumbling and complaining than almost anything else in life. Such, however, should not be the attitude of the Christian. Yet even saints grumble and complain about the weather, as if the Creator did not know His own business. No matter what kind of a day it is, the saint should say, *"This is the day which the LORD hath made; we will rejoice and be glad in it"* (Psalm 118:24). Learn to carry the sunshine in your heart; then you will be independent of it whether or not you have it outside.

We are discontented with the success of others. Jealousy breeds discontent and such a sin needs to be stamped out among God's people. If another is elevated or raised and we are left behind (especially if we think ourselves more worthy of the position), the spirit of discontent is quickly generated. No matter how such a spirit is caused, we need to be saved from it. We need to live on the victory side, as Paul could do, otherwise he would never have written, *"I have learned, in whatsoever state I am, therewith to be content"* (Philippians 4:11).

The Tyranny of Temper. What an ugly fruit of sin unholy anger or the uncontrolled temper is! How the manifestation of it hinders the work of the gospel! When we say and do things in a sudden outburst of passion, it brings disgrace to our Lord. It was temper that cost Moses, the meekest of men, a lonely grave on Mount Nebo and the forfeiture of the privilege of entering Canaan. Yet the words of anger, the hastiness of passion, and temper dog the footsteps of the best saints, sometimes giving them sorrow of heart and destroying their influence over others.

If such a sin is ours, let us not listen to the false philosophy about mastering our temper. The wolf is too ferocious for the flesh to tame. We must let Christ convert it, thereby pouring our ungovernable passions into right channels. When we are tempted to get too heated and feel our passions rising, let us turn immediately to the Savior and pray, "Thy tranquility, O Lord!" *"The fruit of the Spirit…is temperance"* (Galatians 5:22–23), that is, temper under His divine control, not merely under self-control.

The Bondage of Self-Consciousness. Often God's people need salvation from the self-life, the outstanding phase of such being self-consciousness. *"Keep back thy servant also from presumptuous sins"* (Psalm 19:13). We are self-conscious in respect to our gifts, abilities, our possessions, and we are apt to become too self-impressed and conceited. We are guilty of self-sufficiency, self-advertisement, and self-glory. It is "I," not "Christ." Sometimes we are too self-conscious in gatherings for prayer or witness and need to be saved from the dumb demon possessing us. We refrain from opening our lips because of the thoughts of others. It is a sin to be silent when we are urged to open our lips. It is also a sin to speak when we should be silent. Some need to be saved from a silent church formalism and made more outwardly aggressive and active regarding the souls of others.

The Spirit of Drudgery in Service. Another sin, all too common among Christians, is the lack of freshness, joy, and exuberance in service. There is no anointing with fresh oil. One forces oneself to do certain things simply because it is expected. People get into a groove and say, "Oh, I suppose I must go to church," as if such an action was something most distasteful. There is no real heart in doing the King's business, no joy, delight, or alacrity in serving the Lord. *"Thou servedst not the* Lord *thy God with joyfulness, and with gladness of heart"* (Deuteronomy 28:47). If this is your spirit, perhaps some forbidden thing is robbing you of that fresh, warm interest you used to have in His most blessed cause. Drudgery God will not have! There is no "pressmen" in His service. Drudgery is sin in a child of God. Oh, for less drudgery and more delight in following Him!

The Plaudits of Men. When we accept the Savior by the definite act of faith in the hour of regeneration, it is essential to realize that the old nature is not removed. Christ dealt with the vital principle of sin at His cross. It was there He broke its power, and He now waits to apply the victory in our lives. Yet one sin, with remaining entrails, needing to be put in the place of death, is the love of praise and the plaudits of others. We like people to think us kind, loving, generous, and holy. How we need to be saved from the subtle snare of seeking the approbation of others! We profess to be humble, but if we are not given our place, we soon assert our rights for due recognition, reward, and respect. The old nature loves to feed on what others think of us. We are unwilling to serve God independent of whether we receive praise or blame, hate or honor, cheers or jeers. We need to be saved from caring about our reputation. As long as our characters are right, why trouble about our reputations? God will take care of them. It is for us to stand complete in His will and leave the issues of our witness with Him.

The Sin of Doubt. Examining again the covenant people of Israel, we find the doubt and unbelief robbed them of God's highest and best. It is recorded that they could not enter the Promised Land because of unbelief. Jesus also marveled at the doubt of others. Yes, doubt is one of the deep-rooted sins from which we need to be saved daily by the Lord Jesus, the Savior for saints. For example, we doubt whether He can fully save and sanctify us, making our lives blissfully victorious. We fail to claim the heritage of the saints. We doubt whether He can take up our ordinary lives and do great things with and through them. We doubt whether He is able to meet the needs of our personal, home, business, or even church life; can He satisfy our hearts apart from worldly pleasures and pursuits?

Thus Jesus waits to save us: to give us radiancy of faith. O what a Savior and what a salvation! But are they ours experimentally? Are we fully saved? If conscious of our sins and failures, will we let Him cleanse us, yes, even us, from our sins? Can we sing, "Jesus saves me all the time, and Jesus saves me now"?

Paul was confident of this very thing: the God who had begun the good work of salvation in the hearts of the Philippians was able to perform or perfect it until the day of Jesus Christ. Oh, saints of God, let us be satisfied with nothing less than this fresh and full salvation!

> Love perfecteth what it begins,
> His power doth save me from my sins,
> His grace upholdeth me.
> —J. S. Piggott

Take heed to the exhortation:

> *Therefore, my dear friends, as you have always obeyed—not only in my presence, but now much more in my absence—continue to work out your salvation with fear and trembling, for it is God who works in you to will and to act in order to fulfill his good purpose. Do everything without grumbling or arguing, so that you may become blameless and pure, children of God without fault in a crooked and warped generation, in which will shine like stars in the universe.*
>
> (Philippians 2:12–15 NIV)

He is able to fully save us, but only, however, as we exercise a continuous faith in the divine ability to keep us from falling. As James Smith, Bible expositor of an earlier generation, expressed it:

> The Lord hath saved us, and He will save us even to the end. He has power, and He will exert it; He has authority, and He will employ it; He has sympathy, and He will manifest it; He is ready, and will deliver. Has He not proved Himself in our past

experience, and ought we not to trust Him for the future?...the Lord waits to save us. Let us believe, and be happy. He will save, He will rest in His love, and joy over us with singing.

"God Will Take Care of You"

Be not dismayed whate'er betide, God will take care of you;
Beneath His wings of love abide, God will take care of you.
God will take care of you,
Through every day, o'er all the way;
He will take care of you, God will take care of you.
—*Civilla D. Martin*, 1904

9

COMFORT ENCOURAGES FELLOWSHIP

"Comfort one another."
—1 Thessalonians 4:18

"Therefore encourage one another and build each other up,
just as in fact you are doing."
—1 Thessalonians 5:11 (NIV)

It is impossible to read the Acts and the epistles without realizing how the early Christians exhibited a fellowship of "kindred minds, like to that above."[2] Their hearts were bound as one in Christian love. Their unanimity of thought, faith, and purpose is most striking. A conspicuous word in Acts, occurring some twelve times, is *accord*, meaning likeminded. When they gathered together for worship and witness, it was with one accord, implying not a mere coming together at a given time and in a certain place, but unity in agreement and aim.

As a result of Pentecost, the disciples were fused into one body and became joined together in soul and sentiment. They revealed a unity of life in love. Any effort to destroy such unity was immediately and drastically dealt with (as in the case of the planned deception of Ananias and Sapphira). An intimate relationship existed among believers as if they were members of one household which, in reality, they were. These

2. John Fawcett, "Blest Be the Tie That Binds" (1782).

early believers were part of the household of God. Frequent exhortations and precepts appear in Acts and the epistles such as, *"Let brotherly love continue"* (Hebrews 13:1), and *"Keep the unity of the Spirit in the bond of peace"* (Ephesians 4:3). Paul, whose ministry was far-reaching in the consolidation of the early church into the fellowship of the Spirit, wrote to the Philippians,

> *Then make my joy complete by being like-minded, having the same love, being one in spirit and purpose. Do nothing out of selfish ambition or vain conceit, but in humility consider others better than yourselves. Each of you should look not only to your own interests, but also to the interests of others.*   (Philippians 2:2–4 NIV)

All these admonitions impress one with the solidarity of the growing church. Positionally, the believers were all *"one in Christ Jesus"* (Galatians 3:28 NIV), and their goal was to present such accord practically before the world.

While we have noted several evidences of such spiritual oneness, it is not generally understood that comfort was one of them. Yet there is ample proof that mutual consolation was a vital, binding influence in the cementing of first-century saints into one body or building (both terms are used of the church). The divine Comforter indwelling them revealed Himself in the ministry of comfort He inspired in the early church.

In Paul's epistle to the Romans he expressed the request *"that I may be comforted together with you by the mutual faith both of you and me"* (Romans 1:12). Oneness in comfort is also emphasized in the apostle's principles of action.

> *Whether we be afflicted...or whether we be comforted, it is for your consolation and salvation.*   (2 Corinthians 1:6)

> *Forgive him, and comfort him.*   (2 Corinthians 2:7)

> *I am filled with comfort, I am exceeding joyful in all our tribulation.*   (2 Corinthians 7:4)

We were comforted in your comfort. (2 Corinthians 7:13)

Paul and the saints he nurtured knew how to prevail in prayer, hence the firm unity that marked their witness. To those Paul had never seen in the flesh he could write, *"Their hearts might be comforted, being knit together in love"* (Colossians 2:2), *"My fellowworkers...have been a comfort to me"* (Colossians 4:11), and *"Wherefore comfort one another"* (1 Thessalonians 4:18; see 2 Thessalonians 2:17). Are not these passages sufficient to indicate that the early church laid stress upon comfort in all phases of its meaning, such as sympathy, consolation, cheer, encouragement, strength, and exhortation? When Job was struck down, his three friends came to mourn with him and comfort him. For seven days and nights they sat in solitude with Job. Yet Job came to say, *"Comfort ye me in vain,"* and was forced to call them *"miserable comforters"* because their comfort was not in love, sincerity, and truth (Job 2:11; 16:2; 21:34). How different was the comfort that bound the hearts of Paul and his friends in a blessed fellowship!

Applying these facts to the church of today, we are told in no uncertain terms (both by religious and non-religious writers) that shortcomings and blemishes are making the church a less potent force in the world. It is all too evident the church has drifted from the earnest contention for *"the faith which was once delivered unto the saints"* (Jude 3). The early church, because of its unswerving devotion to the faith, was able to build one another up in their *"most holy faith"* and show compassion for others, as well as experience deliverance from sin and error (Jude 20–24). Congregations may lustily sing on a Sunday morning,

> We are not divided,
> All one body we—
> One in hope and doctrine,
> One in charity.
> —*Sabine Baring-Gould*

For far too many, this is a lie. The fact remains that they are not "one body," as Paul understood the mystic phrase. Too often, a church is made up of members by application, who become only units, or a group of individuals, with varying and opposite views of Scripture. They are not one in hope and doctrine, and consequently, not one in love. Spiritual unity is lacking. There is an absence of that agreement of soul and sentiment so prominent in the early church. Wherever you have a group of church members who are not one in hope and doctrine, you have those who are not one in charity or love. Because of this absence of mutual love, there is, as a result, the absence of actual comfort. Think of what would happen in any given church if its members gave themselves to comfort one another in the full sense of consolation, cheer, and encouragement! What a binding influence this would provide, making the given church one loving family!

It is unfortunate that we are guilty of criticizing or condemning one another, rather than comforting one another with the promises of God. Hearts are not bound in Christian love. Mutual burdens are not borne and for each other there does not flow the sympathizing tear, as the hymn expresses it. Charles Wesley emphasizes what it means to function as the Lord's "mystic body" and to be "in one spirit joined":

> Sweetly may we all agree,
> Touched with loving sympathy;
> Kindly for each other care;
> Every member feel its share.

May the Head of the body enable us in church life and work to imitate Him as the One who came to comfort all who mourn and to cultivate a spirit of love to all saints, notwithstanding their weaknesses, exercising forbearance and pity. May we be slow to anger and ready to forgive, accepting the will for the deed. May we be always ready to exhibit the consolations of Christ in trouble or distress.

> "It is a little thing to speak a phrase of common comfort,
> which by daily use has almost lost its sense;
> and yet, on the ear of him who thought to die unmourned,
> it will fall like the choicest music."
> —*Talfourd*

10

COMFORT FOR BROKEN HEARTS

"Scorn has broken my heart and has left me helpless; I look for sympathy, but there was none, for comforters, but I found none."
—Psalm 69:20 (NIV)

"He has sent me to bind up the brokenhearted, to proclaim freedom for the captives."
—Isaiah 61:1 (NIV)

Sorrow in some form follows us from cradle to grave. None escapes its pang. More than ever, the world is sorrow-stricken. Our comfort is that Jesus came to heal the brokenhearted. (See Luke 4:18.) One of the sweetest hymns Charles Wesley wrote was "Thou Hidden Source of Calm Repose," in which he exalts Christ as being all sufficient. He is our rest in toil, our ease in pain, our peace in conflict, our gain in loss, our liberty in bondage, our heaven in hell.

There was a Christian who constantly conducted great business transactions. Although he was surrounded by overwhelming responsibilities, he was always calm and serene. Asked how he was able to preserve tranquility of mind amid all his cares, he replied, "By making Christ my all in all." After a time he sustained heavy losses, yet in his commercial crises he was as calm as ever. Asked again how he could possibly maintain cheerfulness at such a time, he said, "By finding my all in Christ."

Wesley's great hymn teaches us to make Christ our all in all and to find our all in Him. There is a line that caught this writer's eye and fires his imagination. It is in the third stanza where Charles Wesley speaks of Jesus as the "medicine for my broken heart." Suggestive, is it not? It indicates that the whole world is a universal hospital, and Christ's practice as the Great Physician is a large one. The different nations are like separate wards of a vast hospital.

How sad we feel as we walk through a hospital and find men and women broken in body, or visit a mental institution and see people broken in mind. In a prison, those broken in character will be found. Yet what must God see as He looks down and beholds those who are broken in body, in mind, or in character in all the nations of the world? A brilliant German skeptic said to a Christian worker, "If I could see what God sees, it would break my heart." The reply he received was, "God's heart did break at Calvary." It was there He provided a remedy for all the sores, sins, and sorrows of humanity. Dr. Joseph Parker's advice to young preachers was "preach to broken hearts." We have a need to do so, for the world is full of them.

The word the Bible uses for brokenhearted means *to break in pieces*, conveying the idea of helplessness, uselessness, and inertia. It is used of an animal being torn apart by wild beasts or a ship broken by the storm. It is descriptive of an organ of the body not merely full of ache and suffering, but while it aches, is also helpless and utterly unable to do what is required of it.

If an arm is struck a sudden blow, it hangs useless and pain-gripped. When overtaken by sudden calamity, we are not only heartbroken, but useless, inert. Some forms of intense suffering act as a stimulant. They arouse us to new energy, but when brokenhearted we are unable to do anything but suffer. Apart from the aid of the divine Healer, we are hopeless. Is it not blessed to know when disaster overtakes us and the heart is robbed of its strength, there is One so near to the broken heart? Why, the very helplessness constitutes an appeal to the heart of the heavenly Comforter! With those perfect, unerring hands of His, He binds up the wounded spirit.

Literally, as well as figuratively, people are brokenhearted. They are worn-out by business and excessive toil, shocked by heavy and humiliating losses, wakened by wearying and trying sicknesses, distressed over terrible bereavement, and disappointed because of the cruel treachery of friends. Yes, each life has its own heartaches. *"Reproach hath broken my heart"* (Psalm 69:20).

The evil of sin also affects the heart. We shed bitter tears over our failures. Shame and anguish are ours as we think of our rebellion against God's will. We are heartbroken over our ingratitude and rejection of God's best for our lives. Paul said, *"O wretched man that I am!"* (Romans 7:24). The heart is wounded by the stinging power of the Serpent's fang. We live in a proud age when it is not fashionable to be brokenhearted over sin—our own, or another's. What need we have to rend the heart and find the Lord is gracious. (See Amos 5:15.) May the Word of God, as a hammer, fall upon our rock-like hearts until broken by blows, we turn to the Balm of Gilead!

Shakespeare put the question on the lips of Macbeth, "Canst thou not minister to a mind diseased?" How grateful we are for the Lord who can mend broken hearts! What a perfect Physician He is! His own heart was broken, and His wounds supply the medicine our broken, bleeding hearts require. He heals by offering the most tender sympathy. It is of great importance for a physician to have a good bedside manner. Jesus is troubled with all the feelings of our infirmities. He can enter into our grief of mind and body. Our Lord is able to come alongside in our life, as the physician may stand at the bed of his patient, and feel our pulse and prescribe a fitting remedy.

He also heals by ministering divine comfort. Who else is able to exercise such a delicate ministry? Human comforters are sometimes clumsy. They hurt rather than heal, but Christ knows how to cause the gentle dew of comfort to cool the fevered spirit.

He heals, too, whenever He grants us effectual help. The most skilled of earth sometimes fail. Trajan died in the hands of his court physician. Over his tomb they wrote, "Here lies Trajan, the Emperor, that may thank his physician that he died." How different it is with

Jesus! His skill is infallible. When His advice and His medicine are sought, He never fails to heal the broken heart. He has never lost a patient.

The story is told of an old heathen woman who came to a native medicine shop to buy medicine. While her medicines were being prepared, a missionary entered and noticed the old woman, sad and unhappy in appearance. When asked the reason for her downcast look, the woman replied that last year her husband had died and now her son was ill and about to die. "Why," said the missionary, "what you need is not drugs but comfort. You should go across the street to the Mission Hall where they have medicine for broken hearts."

Yes, the Lord is able to heal the brokenhearted. But we must be conscious of our deep need. *"They that be whole need not a physician"* (Matthew 9:12). When our heartaches draw us to the heavenly Physician, remedy becomes ours through the Cross, the Holy Spirit, the Word, and also through the sympathetic ministry of others.

If we are bruised and broken by sin, God has a healing message of free and full forgiveness for us. By His stripes we are healed. The joy of acceptance and the welcome of love become ours by the blood of the cross. As the Good Samaritan, He binds up the bleeding wounds which sin has caused, applying the ointment of grace on the soft bandages of love.

If we are broken by the misdeeds of others, even by professing Christians or by so-called friends, or crushed by the sorrows and cares of life, the Lord is at hand to heal our wounds. Let us not hesitate to uncover our gaping wound. Tenderly He can heal. His skillful hands never fail to bind up the broken heart.

> What a Friend we have in Jesus, all our sins and griefs to bear!
> What a privilege to carry everything to God in prayer.
> Can we find a Friend so faithful? Who will all our sorrows share?
> Jesus knows our ev'ry weakness—
> Take it to the Lord in prayer.
> —*Joseph Scriven*

"God, give us grace to accept with serenity the things that cannot be changed, courage to change the things that should be changed, and the wisdom to distinguish the one from the other."
—*Reinhold Niebuhr*

11

COMFORT WHEN GOD SEEMS FAR AWAY

"Certainly I will be with thee."
—Exodus 3:12

"Lo, I am with you always, even to the end of the age."
—Matthew 28:20 (NASB)

"He hath said, I will never leave thee, nor forsake thee."
—Hebrews 13:5

There is an oft-recurring promise of the Old Testament used in different connections: "I will never leave you." We find it, first of all, made by God to Jacob at Bethel. The very same promise was handed on to Joshua and the people of God by Moses, as Moses was about to leave them. Then in Joshua's own last charge to the Israelites, we find the promise repeated again. When David left Solomon instructions regarding the building of the temple, he also told his son that God would not leave him or forsake him. In the epistle to the Hebrews we have the promise for our own daily provision and comfort, *"Let your conversation be without covetousness; and be content with such things as ye have: for he hath said, I will never leave thee, nor forsake thee"* (Hebrews 13:5).

In this verse we have three precious things bound together by the divine Spirit. First, there is conversation without covetousness: *"Let your conversation be without covetousness."* Then we have contentment amid all circumstances: *"Be content with such things as ye have."* Finally, there is the companionship of Christ. *"For He has said, I will never leave thee nor forsake thee." "What therefore God hath joined together, let not man put asunder"* (Matthew 19:6).

May we experience what it is to have conversation without covetousness! We are forever sinning in this direction; we covet what some people have or what other people wear. Paul declared that he would never have known the law had it not said, *"Thou shalt not covet"* (Romans 7:7). Then there is contentment in the adverse circumstances of life. *"Be content with such things as ye have." "Godliness with contentment is great gain"* (1 Timothy 6:6). One of our prevailing sins is that of discontentment, and yet we are enjoined by the Holy Spirit to be content with the things we have.

Such a verse would mock us if it finished there. It is difficult indeed for some people to be content with such things as they have. We think of the many who are upon beds of pain and physical weakness, of others who find themselves in difficult circumstances. Going up to such men and women in these days of stress and strain, we would hurt their feelings if we said, "You must be content with such things as you have." But the verse goes on to say, *"He hath said, I will never leave thee nor forsake thee."* There is the secret of true contentment, namely, realizing the companionship of the Lord Jesus. If we realize that He is ever near, "the secret source of every precious thing," then we can have conversation without covetousness and contentment in the adverse circumstances of life.

Making his pastoral visits one day, a minister came in contact with a Christian woman who was very poor indeed. He found her living all alone in a miserable attic. In her room there was a complete absence of comfort, and the minister could see that this dear saint of God was having a struggle to make ends meet. Sitting down beside her somewhat bare table, he noticed a dry crust of bread upon a plate. Speaking gently to this lonely woman who knew the Lord, the minister asked: "Do you mean to tell me that this is all you have in the house?" Her reply came swiftly, "No, I have the crust and Christ." She knew by having Christ as well as the crust, she would find the next meal forthcoming. Isaiah 35:4 tells us, *"Be strong, fear not: behold, your God…will come and save you,"* reminding us of the words of an unknown poet,

"Fear not, I am with thee";
Blessed golden ray, Like a star of glory,
Lighting up my way.
Through the clouds of midnight,
This bright promise shone,
I will never leave thee, Never leave thee alone.

Here, then, is one of the most precious promises contained in the Word of God. There are two outstanding things to consider, namely, the Promiser and the Promise.

THE PROMISE MAKER

Think of the one who made this promise in Hebrews 13:5. Notice the emphasis upon the pronoun. The writer is not telling us what he had experienced regarding the companionship of the Lord; he is not giving his testimony. It is the Lord speaking for Himself. As we have it in the RV, *"Himself hath said, I will never leave thee, I will never forsake thee."* The character of a person has a good deal to do with the fulfillment of any promise He may make. We have many friends who make promises, but we never look for a realization of them; we happen to know the Promisers! William Hazlitt said, "Some men make promises that they may have the pleasure of breaking them." Not so of the Lord Jesus. *"He is faithful that promised"* (Hebrews 10:23). Here is the divine Promiser, *"Himself hath said,"* and because of who He is, we know He will fulfill the promise that He Himself made. Have you noticed that whether you read this promise the right way or backwards, it means the same? Here it is back to front: "Thee forsake never will I, thee leave never will I."

THE PROMISE NOT TO FORSAKE YOU

Then we have His promise. "*I will never leave you, nor forsake you.*" These two parts of the promise carry with them a twofold thought. They do not mean the same thing. The Holy Spirit was never guilty of tautology when the Spirit made possible the Word of God. In these two phrases we have two wonderful truths for our hearts. In the first expression, the Lord assures us that He will never withdraw His guiding hand, and in the second, that He will never withdraw His protecting presence.

His presence is promised to His people, even though He is not always perceived by sense.

Unfailing Companion. Look at the first part of the promise, "*I will never leave thee,*" or, as we have it in the RV, "*I will in no way fail thee.*" The Promiser presents Himself as the unfailing Companion. Others fail us. We have those who fail us because of sin, sickness, or death, but amid all the failures of life there stands upon the pilgrim way this unfailing One. Dr. Weymouth tells us that the inner meaning of the promise is "I will never, never let go of your hand." Although living and loving hands are forced to release their pressure on our hand, we are guided and directed by the hand of the Lord, which never releases its hold. God's hand will continue to lead and provide until traveling days are done, and when we get to the end of our journey, that same hand will guide us from the dusty lanes of earth to the gold streets above.

In the second part of the promise, we have the constant companionship of the Promiser Himself, not only His provision, but His Person. This word *forsake* really means "to leave behind in any state or place." The Lord has promised never to leave us behind in any state or place.

He Neither Leaves, Nor Forsakes Us. Now let us take these two phrases and look at them from different angles. "I will never, never leave you; I will never forsake you." First, it is possible to be *forsaken and yet not left.* Some time ago there was a tragedy in a certain home. It was caused by the estrangement between husband and wife. Another woman had come into the life of the husband, and his wife was heartbroken. They were living together beneath the same roof but had very little companionship with one another. The husband had forsaken the wife, but he had not left her. Thus it was possible for her to be forsaken and yet not left.

There are many who have determined to follow the Lord all the way and after declaring their allegiance to Him, have come to understand what it means to follow Him and to function as true disciples. Some live in a home where there are others having no sympathy with spiritual things. The rest of the family walks the broad road, but there are those who are truly consecrated, striving to follow the Savior on the narrow path. There is little sympathy, but, of course, those devoted souls wisely continue to live at home, so their lives may tell upon those around them. Those in the home who love the ways of the world treat the consecrated souls with contempt; they ostracize them. They have forsaken them, but have not left them.

Then it is possible to be *left and yet not forsaken*. Years ago I had to leave home on my preaching missions. It was always a sad farewell, but although I left my home, I did not forsake it. Most of us have loved ones serving God far from home. They determined to dedicate their lives to the Lord and to follow the gleam. Today, in some distant part of the world, they are giving their all for God. They left their homes, but did not forsake them.

The dead have left us, and our homes have been emptied of their treasures. We have half our heart in heaven. It is blessed to know they are with the Lord; He leads and guides them with His right hand. As we linger in the shadows, He guides and directs us with His hand. He is ever between and although the dead have left us, we know they have not forsaken us. Before long—it may be sooner than we expect—we will experience a blessed reunion.

Also, it is possible to be *left and forsaken*. I know of nothing so distressing. From the early years of my ministry I remember entering a home where it was difficult to give advice. A heartbroken woman lived there. Some two or three years prior to my visit, her husband had made up his mind to leave England and go out to one of the colonies. He left his wife and children behind with the promise that he would strive in every possible way to make money in order to send for them. His wife did not know that when he left home he was ceasing to care for her. For some two or three years she had received no letters from him, not even a cent for her support or the sustenance of his children. She had truly been left and forsaken.

There is One who stands before us and declares He will *never leave us, nor forsake us.* No matter how we may love each other, we are never in the presence of our dearest friends every part of every day, but here is One who declares He will never leave us, never forsake us.

We Forsake Him. Yet what the Lord will never do, alas, we ourselves are all too capable of doing. There may be times when we feel He has left and forsaken us, but let us never mistake our feelings for actualities.

Because of trial and adversity, we may feel as though the Lord is no longer near, but in the darkest hour let us believe his promise, "*I will never, never leave thee; I will never forsake thee.*" It maybe, however, that the fault is in ourselves, for we both leave and forsake the Lord. "*My people have committed two sins: They have forsaken me, the spring of living water, and have dug their own cisterns, broken cisterns that cannot hold water*" (Jeremiah 2:13 NIV). The Word of God reminds us of some things that can lead us to leave and forsake the abiding Companion.

I wonder if we have ever thought of bringing two passages of Holy Writ together. We find them at the beginning and at the end of our Lord's ministry. At the beginning of His ministry we read, "*They forsook all, and followed him*" (Luke 5:11). That was a remarkable surrender. These men who heard His voice by the Sea of Galilee forsook all and followed Him. At the end of His ministry, when those selfsame men understood something of the cost of discipleship, we read, "*They all forsook him, and fled*" (Mark 14:50). The soldiers came out against Jesus with swords and staves and when the disciples saw them, they forsook Jesus and fled, deserting the very One for whom they had forsaken all things.

Persecution often leads men and women to forsake the Lord. When they discover that following Christ means identification with Him in His shame and sacrifice, then they are unwilling to pay the price. We have seen many make a profession of faith during a special evangelistic effort. Then they find themselves out in the cold, bare world, brought up against the stern fact that Jesus does not call them to travel over an easy road. Discipleship means complete identification with Him in His death. Then, alas, they forsake Him. Like the disciples, they flee.

Again, there is no experience in the New Testament more poignant than the life of the apostle Paul, who was so like His Master in respect to the sufferings he endured. As an old man, and although such a remarkable saint, he yet realized the need of human companionship. He had a friend who was ever near and whose presence soothed and consoled him in many of his dark hours. One day he needed a friend and reached out that he might feel something of the grasp of a loving, sympathetic hand. It was not there, and thus the apostle had to write, *"Demas hath forsaken me, having loved this present world"* (2 Timothy 4:10). It does not say "this present evil world" as we sometimes misquote the passage, but "having loved this present world." Because of the fascination of things, Demas was tempted to leave and forsake his bosom companion. I wonder if the Lord is looking down from glory today, saying, as He thinks of the many who once named His name, "They have forsaken me, having loved this present world"?

We find Him where we left Him. Are these lines being read by one who has abandoned Christ upon his conscience? Are you living with the realization that you have left and forsaken the abiding Lord? You can once again realize the nearness of the Lord. If you have left Jesus, you will find Him where you left Him.

His own mother, Mary, had to learn this. In the excitement of things on that trip to Jerusalem, she forgot about the boy Jesus. She left Him behind in the temple and went on with her friends. While journeying home, she became conscious that Jesus was not with her. As we read, *she* sought for Him among her kinfolk and acquaintances. But He was not with them. She found Jesus where she had left Him. She had to journey back to the temple and found the Lord Jesus in the midst of the learned men, asking and answering questions. (See Luke 2:41–50.) We always find Jesus where we leave Him.

I think of a dear lady who came to me at the close of a service. In deep distress of mind, she told me she had lost her joy. She had no power in her witness. For some time, something like nine months, she had been living under a cloud. She asked me to help her in spiritual matters; she wanted once again to bask in the sunshine of the Savior's presence. I asked, "Can you tell me what happened nine months ago? Then possibly I can help you. Why was it you lost your joy?"

"The only thing I can remember," she said, "is that about nine months ago we had a rummage sale in our church (one of those wretched things that some churches sponsor these days to keep the machinery going, as if God were too poor to look after His business). I had a stall at the sale and next to me there was another member of the church who also had a stall. I think we became rather jealous of each other and, in an unguarded moment, I said something to her, and words passed between us. Since that day we have never spoken to each other. We still go to the same church. Although for nine months I have seen her every Sunday, we yet leave the church and do not speak."

"Well," I said, "You will find Jesus just where you left Him."

"What do you mean by that?" the lady asked.

"If you know you were wrong, you must see that sister and make amends; you must apologize. If she is near at hand, you must see her tonight. If she is away, you must write to her, and, in the spirit of Jesus say you are sorry. You must seek her forgiveness, and the moment you put that matter right, believe me, you will find Jesus—where you left Him!"

She came back a few days later. I could see by her countenance that she had found her Lord again. She had gone home and put the matter right, and with restitution there came the restoration of joy, peace, and power. Yes, Jesus never leaves us. If we leave Him, we always find Him just where we left Him.

Oh, what a gracious promise. *"I will never leave you; I will never forsake you!"* We cannot read these words, falling as they did from the lips of our blessed Lord Himself, without realizing they drip with His own heart's blood. There at Calvary, as His mangled form was stretched upon the tree, He cried, *"My God, my God, why hast thou forsaken me?"* (Matthew 27:46). He was forsaken in that lone hour that He might have grace to say to His redeemed people, *"I will never leave you; I will never forsake you."*

Not 'till the loom is silent
And the shuttles cease to fly
Shall God unroll the canvas
And explain the reason why
The dark threads are as needful
In the weaver's skillful hand
as the threads of gold and silver
In the pattern He has planned.
—*Author Unknown*

12

COMFORT IN DISTRESS

"When Job's three friends, Eliphaz the Temanite, Bildad the Shuhite and Zophar the Naamathite, heard about all the troubles that had come upon him, they set out from their homes and met together by agreement to go and sympathize with him and comfort him."
—Job 2:11 (NIV)

"This is why I weep and my eyes overflow with tears. No one is near to comfort me, no one to restore my spirit. My children are destitute because the enemy has prevailed."
— Lamentations 1:16 (NIV)

"Why are you downcast, O my soul? Why so disturbed within me? Put your hope in God, for I will yet praise him, my Savior and my God."
—Psalm 42:11 (NIV)

"For just as the sufferings of Christ flow over into our lives, so also through Christ our comfort overflows."
—2 Corinthians 1:5 (NIV)

"And our hope for you is firm, because we know that just as you share in our sufferings, so also you share in our comfort."
—2 Corinthians 1:7 (NIV)

The evil-driven world in which we live, with its acute international and national crises and problems, is responsible for the creeping paralysis of hopelessness and despair so apparent in the lives of many. For them the struggle to live and of living has become intolerable. They are among those whose spirits are overwhelmed and whose souls refuse to be comforted. (See Psalm 77:2.) Hands hang down, and knees are feeble. (See Hebrews 12:12.) These depressed hearts have given up hope of finding light in darkness, strength in weakness, direction in perplexity, deliverance in danger, victory in conflict, and triumph in life. Three times over the psalmist laments, *"Why are you cast down, O my soul?"* (Psalm 42:5, 11; 43:5 NIV).

Spurgeon rightly asks, "Why this deep depression, this faithless fainting, this chicken-hearted melancholy?" The psalmist was right to rebuke himself and to declare his God was a God of hope, able to bring light out of darkness, straighten crooked things, and make all grace abound for those who felt themselves sinking beneath the waves of trial and pressures. Have we found comfort in distressing situations knowing that the foundation of hope is laid up for us in the blood of Jesus and the oath of God? The injunction of old was *"Let Israel hope in the LORD"* (Psalm 130:7)—hope in His mercy, in His patience, in His provision, and in His plenteous grace.

> Why restless, why cast down, my soul?
> Hope still, and thou shalt sing
> The praise of Him who is thy God,
> Thy health's eternal spring.
> —*Author Unknown*

HOPE FOR RELIEF IN DISTRESS

God has spoken, and He is true and faithful. He cannot disappoint your expectations. Changes in life may result in despair, but they cannot affect Him who is without change. Amid circumstances conspiring to rob you of peace, say to your forlorn heart, "I will hope in God who is all-gracious and all-powerful, and I will trust Him to do all a loving Father and infinite God can do for me in my dilemma!" After chiding his soul for its misery, David cried, "*I shall yet praise him*" (Psalm 42:5). Future believers would follow his example of hoping in God's character in the midst of distressing circumstances.

Among those imprisoned in Canterbury Castle for their faith in Christ was a noble woman, Alice Benden. By the bishop's order, she was let down into a deep dungeon where none of her friends could come to her. Her bed was a little straw, between a pair of stocks and a stone wall. As she lay there she asked herself why her Lord allowed her to suffer this way, so far from her friends. As she wallowed in self-pity, she began repeating to herself the words of the psalmist, "Why art thou so heavy, O my soul, and why art thou so cast down within me? Still trust in God," she said, "God's hand can change all this." This gave her comfort in her sorrow, and she continued to be joyful until she was released.

In an autobiographical message, Cardinal Henry Manning also quoted David saying, "'*Why art thou cast down, O my soul*' was always a delight to me." Every day in daily Mass the verse comes back to me. How expressive of our own feelings this same verse has been when we have felt somewhat low in spirit! Those Bohemian martyrs who suffered at Prague in 1621 found comfort in the Psalms as they died for the Lord. For instance, when one of the martyrs, John Schultis, reached the scaffold, he said, "Why art thou cast down, O my soul? Hope thou in God for I shall yet praise Him. The righteous seem in the eyes of men to die, but indeed they go to their rest." Then kneeling down he cried, "Come, come, Lord Jesus, do not tarry."

Martin Luther, who clung to the Psalter as a tried and trusted friend, had moments when he felt something akin to despair. At times he lamented with David, "*Why art thou cast down, O my soul?*" It was in such hours that he would say to his friend Melancthon, "Come, Philip, let us sing Psalm 46!" The message to Israel is surely one for our own hearts, "*Let Israel hope in the* LORD" (Psalm 130:7). Because God is the God of hope, we should hope in Him confidently, for He has promised;

prayerfully, for He loves to hear from us; obediently, for His precepts are to be observed by us; constantly, for He is always the same.

The gospel bears my spirit up;
A faithful and unchanging God
Lays the foundation for my hope,
In oaths, and promises, and blood;
Then, O my soul, still hope in God,
And plead thy Savior's precious blood.
—*Author Unknown*

The patriarch Job reminds us that *"man is born to trouble as surely as the sparks fly upward"* (Job 5:7 NIV), and that is the experience of us all. Trouble, often leading to despair, does not bypass any one of us. But while trouble is ever near, the promises of God and the throne of grace are nearer. Any kind of trouble, if received as His permissive will, endears the divine Comforter Himself to our hearts. Has God not declared that in time of trouble He will hide us? What a load of troubles fell upon David, yet listen to his confession,

> *For in the day of trouble he will keep me safe in his dwelling; he will hide me in the shelter of his tabernacle and set me high upon a rock. Then my head will be exalted above the enemies who surround me; at his tabernacle will I sacrifice with shouts of joy; I will sing and make music to the LORD.* (Psalm 27:5–6 NIV)

We must look at our troubles and trials and say, "These also shall turn to my salvation." Look on the past and acknowledge, "Goodness and mercy have followed me." Look to the future and rejoice because "The Lord will give that which is good." Look in every direction and say, "I will trust and not be afraid." Despondency should not arise in our hearts, for the Lord is ever on His way to free us from our cares and troubles. *"Behold, thy salvation cometh!"* (Isaiah 62:11). Paul, although troubled on every side, could yet exultingly say, *"I am filled with comfort, I am exceeding joyful in all our tribulation"* (2 Corinthians 7:4). It is only as we triumph in like manner that we are able to comfort other troubled hearts with the comfort with which we have been comforted by God.

Calmer of my troubled heart,
Bid my unbelief depart;
Speak, and all my sorrows cease;
Speak, and all my soul is peace;
And till I Thy glory see,
Help me to believe in Thee.
—*Author Unknown*

When some difficulty overtakes us there is often the tendency to sit down and mourn, to refuse to eat. To the three men who appeared to Abraham in the plains of Mamre, the patriarch offered food saying, "*I will fetch a morsel of bread, and comfort ye your hearts*" (Genesis 18:5). Here, comfort has the thought of being encouraged, heartened, and strengthened. This was also the experience of Saul in his troubles when he refused to eat. (See 1 Samuel 28:23–25.) Josephus, the Jewish historian, speaks of his admiration for the bravery of Saul at this point. Although there was no strength in Saul, and he knew he would soon lose both his life and honor, he would not desert his army. After his meal, Saul resolutely returned to the camp, ready for the conflict awaiting him.

"God Will Take Care of You"

Be not dismayed whate'er betide,
God will take care of you;
Beneath His wings of love Abide,
God will take care of you.

No matter what may be the test,
God will take care of you;
Lean, weary one, upon His breast,
God will take care of you.

God will take care of you,
Through every day, o'er all the way;
He will take care of you,
God will take care of you.
—*Civilla D. Martin*, 1904

13

COMFORT CHEERS THE HEART

"I have seen his ways, but I will heal him; I will guide him."
—Isaiah 57:18 (NIV)

*"Now instead, you ought to forgive and comfort him, so that he
will not be overwhelmed by excessive sorrow."*
—2 Corinthians 2:7 (NIV)

"That I also may be cheered when I receive news about you."
—Philippians 2:19 (NIV)

*"Finally, brothers and sisters, good-by. Aim for perfection, listen to
my appeal, be of one mind, live in peace. And the God of love and
peace will be with you."*
—2 Corinthians 13:11 (NIV)

To many the message of cheer may seem to be a strange note to sound
in days of darkness and sorrow. "How can we be cheerful when there is
so much grief and misery?" one is apt to ask. We are living in a world of
sadness. We are being baptized in the waters of anxiety, suffering, and
death. Each day only adds to the vast army who weeps and mourns. Is

there any room for cheerfulness, when we think about fatherless children, sorrowing widows, and heartbroken parents? Can we be cheerful when we consider the awful carnage, brutality, and horror of wars from which our world is never free?

Yes, we can be cheerful! Moreover our hearts need, and the world needs Christ's message of cheerfulness. He has told us that cheerfulness is possible under every circumstance of life, as we shall discover later on.

Cheerfulness becomes ours when we fix our minds, not upon the discouraging, but upon the encouraging things of life. We never make trouble any the less by thinking about it continually. If we dwell constantly upon our trouble, the molehill will become a mountain, and the note of cheerfulness will be reduced by the noise of sadness. No matter how adverse circumstances may be, there is no cause for despondency. As someone has rightly said, "God is behind all the scenes, and He moves all the scenes He is behind."

After all, the blessings of life outweigh its troubles and sorrows. Take all your discouragements and place them in the scale, weighing them with all the encouragements, and you will find that there are many reasons to be cheerful. Learn to fix your eyes upon the encouragements of life, hide the grief in your own heart, and bear to the outward world a cheerful face and joyful message.

Originally *cheer* was associated with the countenance, the French translation using *chere*, meaning *face*. Then the word came to mean the *expression* on the face, the outward mirror of inner memories, good spirits, and the benediction of a cheerful countenance. *"A merry heart maketh a cheerful countenance"* (Proverbs 15:13). Ultimately the word came to signify good spirits themselves, without any reference to facial expression. Two of the Greek words used for comfort imply cheer up: take heart, feel confident, be of good spirits, and be animated. Thus Paul's exhortation can be freely translated, "That I may cheer up when I know your state." (See Philippians 2:19.)

There is nothing like cheerfulness to dispel the gloom hanging over many lives. It chases the mist away and allows the warm rays of the sun to shine into every dark corner of life. There is a beautiful story told of the Reverend Henry Ward Beecher. One evening as he left his church, he passed two little boys at the door. It was a bitter night and they were almost naked, selling papers to passersby. Beecher put his hands on their heads and gave them a few pennies, saying, "Poor little chaps, aren't you very cold?" And one of them answered, "Yes, sir, we were cold till you passed by." His kindness had warmed them in every way, and believe me, by living the cheerful life, by uttering the cheerful message, you help to warm the sorrow-chilled hearts of many.

Christ's message of cheer was for every circumstance of life. Let us examine now those passages which picture Him cheering the hearts of those who were despondent through varied causes.

FORGIVENESS GIVES CHEER

Take heart, son; your sins are forgiven.   (Matthew 9:2 NIV)

Christ was preaching to a crowd of eager listeners in someone's house, when all at once a palsied man upon his bed was lowered through the flat roof of the house. The four men who had carried him were determined to get him to Jesus. When an entrance was not possible by the door, they ascended the stair, removed a little of the roofing, and lowered their burden down at the Master's feet. When Jesus saw their faith, He said, "Son, be of good cheer."

Possibly that message did not cheer the man as it should have done. The man wanted healing for his body, yet here was Jesus trying to encourage the man by forgiving him his sin. Would it not have cheered the man all the more if Christ had taken him up immediately from his bed of affliction? Yet Christ knew the man, and knew he was suffering because of his sins. The Master flung hope and cheer into the man's heart by giving him what he needed in the first place, forgiveness of sin and cleansing from the past. Then, and not until then, did He deal with the result of his sin. After healing his soul, Jesus proceeded with the body, proving that He is the Divine Physician by healing the man.

The man who came in with his back on the bed went out with the bed on his back.

My friend, has your heart been cheered by such a message? Have you heard the Master say, "My child, be of good cheer, thy sins are forgiven thee"? If not, then know this: your heart is lacking a priceless possession. Pardon comes before every other cleansing. You may crave many needed things from Christ, but you cannot expect them unless and until you have answered His call and allowed Him to heal the plague of your own heart.

Possibly you have the consciousness of your need; you realize you are not right with God. You require no preacher to tell you that you are lost, because your own conscience is your daily preacher. My friend, look not at your sin, for that will only discourage you. Look at Christ and at the provision for your sin and know what it is to have that blessed note sounding in your ears and heart, *"Be of good cheer, thy sins be forgiven thee"* (Matthew 9:2).

ASSURANCE GIVES CHEER

Be of good cheer; it is I; be not afraid.   (Matthew 14:27)

Christ is praying alone upon the mountainside. His disciples are out on the sea where the storms are raging. Their little ship is being tossed about like a cork. The wind is against them, and consequently they can make no progress.

Knowing their dilemma, the Master leaves the mountainside and strides across the troubled waters. Through the darkness and the mist Peter sees his Lord but mistakes Him for a ghost. The whole crew cries out for fear. They are answered and rebuked by Christ's message, *"Be of good cheer; it is I; be not afraid."* Christ practiced what He preached, for He was the most cheerful man of His time, *"anointed…with the oil of gladness above thy fellows"* (Hebrews 1:9).

Encouraged by such a message, Peter wants to leave the boat and walk across to Christ. He is bidden to do so, but on leaving the boat, he looks at the waves and feels the wind. Then he sinks crying, *"Lord, save me"* (Matthew 14:30). Christ raises him up, rebukes him for his little faith, and then enters the boat to calm the troubled waters and hearts.

Surely this is a message for our hearts today. The awful storms of war have broken out upon the world, and waves of sorrow are coming in thick and fast upon human hearts. Our little craft is out upon the angry sea, and it may be that despair is gripping some of our hearts. Are we to sink? Is the storm never to abate? Must we suffer and struggle alone, and after all, go under?

Ah, look! The majestic Christ is walking across the waves to us. He defies the storm and through the mist and darkness there comes His glad message, *"Be of good cheer; it is I; be not afraid."* Yes, let us fix our eyes upon Him, and not upon the gathering storm. When Peter took his eyes from Christ and looked at the storm, the wind, and the waves, he went under, and so do we go under when we allow our circumstances, rather than Christ, to control our lives and fill our vision.

Don't miss the most significant verse in the story. *"When they were come into the ship, the wind ceased"* (Matthew 14:32). Of course it did; it always ceases when the divine Pilot comes on board. Let us not be slow to learn this precious secret when we let the Savior into our hearts, into our boats, we shall be secure for He can control every storm. Moreover, He can dismiss the storm and pour into life, individually, socially, and nationally, the blessed peace of God.

Be of good cheer! We abound with cheer and courage when we know that through all the storms of life Christ is with us. Whether He stills the troubled waves for us or not, He will take care of our boat because He is in it and will guide until it reaches the desired haven. Take courage, troubled heart; Christ is at the helm.

JESUS GIVES CHEER

I have told you these things, so that in me you may have peace. In this world you will have trouble. But take heart! I have overcome the world. (John 16:33 NIV)

Martin Luther said, "This verse is worthy to be carried from Rome to Jerusalem upon one's knee." John 16:33 is indeed a great verse and comes to us like the mighty, heartening shout of a glorious conqueror. Such a cheering message should put to rest every atom of discouragement forevermore. There are three things to notice in this conqueror's cheer.

Tranquility. *"In me...peace."* Christ has been speaking to His disciples about His death and resurrection and also about the dark days that are coming. The Lord will be the Anchor of their souls. Jesus simply explains what the prophet had said: *"Thou wilt keep him in perfect peace"* (Isaiah 26:3). *"In me."* That is our hiding place in every experience of life. Are we in Christ? If we are, then we shall have peace and tranquility.

Tribulation. *"In this world...tribulation."* What opposites we have here. *"In me"*—peace; *"in this world"*—tribulation. Now, if we think we are going to escape tribulation because we are Christians, we have made a great mistake. As long as we are in the flesh and the world, we shall encounter tribulation. Whether it overwhelms us or not depends upon our hiding place. If we are in Him, then a thousand storms may break against us and yet never injure us.

Triumph. *"But take heart! I have overcome the world."* The world with all its dark, evil forces is a defeated foe. Yes, praise God! Notice the past tense of the phrase—*"I have overcome."* Why should we allow the world and all its powers to harass us any longer? Why should we fall before it? Christ has conquered and overcome it; therefore, let us rise and be of good cheer and appropriate Christ's victory over world and the Devil. March on, with His conquering cheer ringing in our hearts, from victory to victory.

ENCOURAGEMENT GIVES CHEER

The Lord stood by him, and said, Be of good cheer, Paul.

(Acts 23:11 SCOFIELD)

If ever Paul needed Christ's message of good cheer, surely it was at this time. He was in Jerusalem making his masterly defense before the

Sanhedrin. The opposition against him was almost unbearable. In fact, at one point Paul forgot himself and called the high priest a *"whited wall"* (Acts 23:3), but afterwards he apologized. Then there arose dissension among the Pharisees and the Sadducees because of Paul's position as a Pharisee. To save him from being mauled to death, the captain of the guard placed Paul in the castle. There the blessed Master came and stood at his side. He encouraged his heart by saying, *"Be of good cheer, Paul."*

In a way, it seemed as if Christ were mocking the feelings of Paul. He certainly needed cheer, but to say that because of his faithful testimony in Jerusalem he would now witness in Rome was enough to discourage the apostle, seeing he would receive far more opposition there. Actually, he would meet his death there.

Nevertheless the apostle was uplifted that his Master saw he was worthy to suffer in such a hard place as Rome because of his faithfulness at Jerusalem. Let us never forget that Jerusalem is before Rome; the only one who can live for Christ at Rome is the one who has passed through Jerusalem undaunted and victorious. How expressive are the lines of Edmund Vance Cooke,

> Oh, a trouble's a ton, or a trouble's an ounce,
> Or a trouble is what you make it.
> And it isn't the fact that you're hurt that counts
> But only, how did you take it.

If you find yourself in a more difficult sphere today than you were some time ago, don't be discouraged. Take cheer from the thought that the Master views you as a valiant conqueror. He has entrusted you with the privilege of witnessing in the most difficult sphere where you may find yourself because of the faithful way in which you served Him elsewhere.

God's hard places are difficult to fill. Rome needs the best saints, but alas, so many fail Him at Jerusalem. If, therefore, we find ourselves in a hard place, let us be of good cheer. God, knowing our past victories, has placed us there.

As noted earlier, cheerfulness is infectious. Paul caught the cheerful spirit of the Master. The message of cheer received that night in the castle nerved him and gave color to all that was before. He went on to Rome to die for his Lord. On the way, you remember, his ship was wrecked. Paul was ready for the occasion. In the midst of the terrific storm he said to the troubled hearts of the others, *"Be of good cheer; for I believe God"* (Acts 27:25). Then he recited all Christ had said that night when He cheered Paul's own heart and went on to give the believing cheer. Moffatt translates this passage, "I now bid you cheer up." May God make us like the apostle! The world needs men and women who are unruffled by the storms of life, who can send out to struggling souls, battling with life's dark waves, the inspiring message, Be of good cheer!

> "Cheerfulness is the principle ingredient in
> the composition of health."
> —*Arthur Murphy*

> "The comforts we enjoy here below, are not like the anchor in
> the bottom of the sea, that holds fast in a storm, but like the
> flag upon the top of the mast, that turns with every wind."
> — *C. Love*

14

COMFORT IN SICKNESS

"My comfort in my suffering is this: Your promise renews my life."
—Psalm 119:50 (NIV)

"Now a man named Lazarus was sick. He was from Bethany, the village of Mary and her sister Martha. This Mary, whose brother Lazarus now lay sick, was the same one who poured perfume on the Lord and wiped his feet with her hair. So the sisters sent word to Jesus, 'Lord, the one you love is sick.'"
—John 11:1–3 (NIV)

"He will wipe every tear from their eyes. There will be no more death or mourning or crying or pain, for the old order of things has passed away."
—Revelation 21:4 (NIV)

Consider our Lord's astonishing dialogue forming part of His Olivet discourse. In it we have reference to six out of the list of the seven corporal works of mercy in Christian ethics, the seventh being the care and nurture of the fatherless. The fifth of these works is impressive: *"I was sick and you visited me"* (Matthew 25:36 RSV). The Greek word visit is a far stronger one than that used of a casual call. It implies a looking after or caring for. But there is no record in the Gospels of Jesus ever being laid aside by sickness and experiencing the loving care of friends.

Since Jesus was sinless He was not subject to any fruit of sin in His own holy body. What He declared in His appealing discourse was that acts of mercy shown toward the needy were ministrations to Himself. *"Inasmuch as ye have done it unto one of the least of these my brethren, ye have done it unto me"* (Matthew 25:40). Here we have, in its highest and most divine form, that exhibition of sympathy and consolation we admire in one of like passions as ourselves. What a difference it would make in our visitations of the sick, if we said to ourselves as we approached the bed of pain, "Ye did it not unto me."

A further instance of Christ's association with sickness is found in John's description of the Bethany home of Mary, Martha, and Lazarus, where Jesus often visited. Deeply distressed about the serious sickness of her brother, Mary sent an urgent appeal to Christ, *"Lord...he whom thou lovest is sick,"* (John 11:3) with the hope that He would hasten to the bedside of the man He loved—to cheer, encourage, and heal him. Jesus did not respond immediately: *"When he had heard therefore that he was sick, he abode two days still...where he was"* (John 11:6). When Jesus ultimately reached Bethany, Lazarus was dead and buried. It must have been trying to the faith of Mary and Martha to have the One they loved act in this way. Love for a sick and dying friend usually prompts speedy help.

When we find ourselves disturbed over a loved one stricken with sickness or disease, we must remember that the ways of divine love are not always the ways of human love. As *Jamieson, Fausset, and Brown's Commentary on the Whole Bible* puts it,

> Often they are the reverse. When His people are sick, in body or spirit; when their case is waxing more and more desperate every day; when all hope of recovery is about to expire—just then and therefore it is that He abides two days still in the same place where He is. Can they still hope against hope? Often they do not; "this is their infirmity." For it is His chosen style of

acting. We have been well taught it, and should not now have the lesson to learn. From the days of Moses was it given sublimely forth as the character of His grandest inter-positions, that *"the* LORD *will judge his people, and repent himself for his servants, when he seeth that their power is gone"* (Deuteronomy 32:36).

It will comfort our hearts as we encounter divine delays that the Lord is never before His time, nor after it. He permitted the sickness of Lazarus to result in death that greater glory might be His. Had he presented Himself immediately at Bethany in response to Mary's appeal, Lazarus would not have died. As Bengel expressed it, "It is beautifully congruous to the divine decorum that in the presence of the Prince of Life no one is ever said to have died." This is the truth beautifully set forth by H. Twells' hymn,

> At even when the sun was set,
> The sick, O Lord, around Thee lay;
> Oh, in what divers pains they met,
> Oh, with what joy they went away.

Our comfort is that as the One alive forevermore, Jesus is the ever-present Helper, not only at the bedside of a loved one who is sick, but in every circumstance of life. "The healing of His seamless dress" is not only "by our beds of pain," but in other experiences requiring His power to heal. He also knows what is best to every child of His in all places, at all times, and under all circumstances. Psalm 147:3 in *The Book of Common Prayer* reads, "He healeth those that are broken in heart; and giveth medicine to heal their sickness, disease, or accident, the sufferer requires all the consolation and cheer a visiting, sympathetic friend can impart."

In one of his wonderful messianic psalms, David gives a delightful and comforting reminder of God's most precious concern for His own people, proving Him to be at hand to encourage in time of need, *"The* LORD *will sustain him on his sickbed and restore him from his bed of illness"* (Psalm 41:3 NIV). Surely that bed must be soft which God will make!

Paxton Hood in *Poets and Poetry of the Bible* tells the story of visiting his beloved friend, Benjamin Parsons, as he lay dying.

> "How are you today?" I asked, and he replied, "My head is sweetly resting on three pillows—infinite power, infinite love, and infinite wisdom." Preaching in Canterbury Hall, Brighton, following this event, and many months after, I was requested to call upon a poor but holy young woman, apparently dying. She said, "I felt I must see you before I died. I heard you tell the story of Benjamin Parsons and his three pillows; and I went through a surgical operation, and it was very hard to bear. But I was leaning my head on the pillows, and as the nurses came to take them away I said, "Mayn't I keep these pillows to ease my pain?" The surgeon, standing by, replied, "No, my dear, we must take them away." "But," said I, "you can't take away Benjamin Parsons' three pillows, I can still lay my head on infinite power, infinite love, and infinite wisdom."

Here, then, is love indeed, when God turns Bed-maker to His sick children. A bed soon becomes hard and disheveled if the body lying in it is tossed to and fro. Grace gives patience, God's smile gives peace, the bed is made to feel soft because the sufferer's heart is content, and the pillows are downy because the head is peaceful. Thomas Fuller tells how Queen Mary of England, when she ignored her evil counselors, accomplished good deeds. For instance, she rebuilt the hospital of the Savoy which had been built by her grandfather Henry VII, and her maids, out of their own wardrobes, furnished it with beds, blankets, and sheets. Fuller adds, "Were any of those ladies still alive, I would pray for them in the language of the Psalmist: '*The* LORD*…make all his bed in his sickness*' (Psalm 41:3). And He is a good bed-maker indeed, who can fit the person and please the patient. But seeing such are all long deceased, it will be no superstition to praise God for their piety, and commend their practice to the imitation of posterity."

There is yet another reference to God's aid as a Physician for those who are sick. "*They that be whole need not a physician, but they that are sick*" (Matthew 9:12). With melancholy in his heart, David came to praise God for becoming the "*health of my countenance*" (Psalm 42:11). The martyr Stephen became so occupied with Jesus that in the midst of his persecutors, as he lay dying, gashed and bleeding from the stone throwing, his face shone as the face of an angel. If our countenance is sad and sickly looking because of an agitated heart, the only way we can shine with the joy of the Lord is to trust and hope in Him and rest in the blessed fact that "*a bruised reed he will not break*" (Matthew 12:20 NIV).

My times are in Thy hand
My God I wish them there
My life my friends my soul I leave
Entirely to Thy care

My times are in Thy hand
Whatever they may be
Pleasing or painful, dark or bright
As best may seem to Thee

My times are in Thy hand
Why should I doubt or fear
A Father's hand will never cause
His child a needless tear

My times are in Thy hand
Jesus the crucified
The hand my cruel sins have grieved
Is now my guard and guide
—*Unknown*

15

COMFORT IN SORROW

*"He is despised and rejected of men; a man of sorrows, and
acquainted with grief....Surely he hath borne our griefs,
and carried our sorrows: yet we did esteem him stricken, smitten
of God, and afflicted. But he was wounded for our transgressions,
he was bruised for our iniquities: the chastisement of our peace was
upon him; and with his stripes we are healed."*
—Isaiah 53:3–5

"O my Comforter in sorrow, my heart is faint within me."
—Jeremiah 8:18 (NIV)

*"'Come and see, Lord,' they replied. Jesus wept. Then the Jews
said, 'See how he loved him!'"*
—John 11:34–36 (NIV)

William Cowper's "The Winter Walk at Noon" reminded us,

There is in souls a sympathy with sound;
And, as a mind is pitch'd the ear is pleas'd
With melting airs, or martial, brisk, or grave;
Some chord in unison with what we hear,
Is touch'd within us, and the heart replies.

Is not Jesus increasingly precious to our hearts as the great High Priest touched with the feeling of our trials and infirmities? Did He not become the *"man of sorrows"* not only because of the sorrows inflicted upon Him, but also in His loving willingness to carry our sorrows?

> In every pang that rends the heart
> The Man of Sorrows shares a part.
> —*Author Unknown*

Here, then, is our consolation when "sorrows like sea billows roll" (Spafford, 1873). In Jesus we have the sympathizing Friend who is ever ready to ease our burden and dry our tears. We say time is a great healer of life's sorrows, but the Man of Sorrows is a greater Healer. He is able to sanctify our sorrows, causing us to be edified and uplifted by them. (See 2 Corinthians 1:5–6.)

Ignorant of the lie that his older sons told about the loss of his much-loved son Joseph, Jacob refused to be comforted by his daughters, believing his son to be dead. He went sorrowing all his days until the great day of discovery came. He learned that his constantly mourned son was alive and was a great ruler in Egypt. What comfort Joseph himself brought to his aged father, as well as to his brothers, even though they had sold him as a slave. (See Genesis 50:15–21.)

While the Jews came to comfort Martha and Mary over the death of their brother, a greater Consoler came to the sorrowing sisters and mingled His tears with theirs. *"Jesus wept"* (John 11:35). He would have us weep with those who weep (see Romans 12:15; Matthew 5:4), and by so doing help to turn their sorrow into joy.

One of the Greek words for comfort carries the idea of *sighing with,* or a *fellow-feeling,* which, says the poet Garrick, "makes us wondrous kind." The most effective consoler is the person who has experienced the very same sorrow or affliction as the one he seeks to comfort. It is here that we distinguish the differences between *sorrow* and *sympathy.* We can have genuine regret for friends facing heartbreak over some trial, disappointment, or illness without any personal knowledge of what they may be passing through—but we cannot have *sympathy* for them unless we have sat where they are sitting. Sympathy is born in the womb of experience. Much comfort often comes from the pressure of a friendly hand and a few simple words, quietly and kindly spoken, such as, "I know just how you feel, for I have been there myself." This was why Ezekiel was such a blessing to the captives in Chaldea, for he was a prisoner himself, and so wrote, *"I sat where they sat"* (Ezekiel 3:15 AMP).

Paul uses an arresting phrase, *"the fellowship of His sufferings"* (Philippians 3:10). This conveys the same idea about a mutual sharing of trials and sorrows. Are we lonely? If so, we can tell Jesus all about our experience, and He will console us. Remember, He had nowhere to lay His head, and all His disciples forsook Him and fled. At the cross, too, there is the mystery too deep for us to understand: He was momentarily forsaken by His Father for our sins. Are we in pain? Jesus can enter with us into such physical anguish for He knew what anticipated pain was, yet went steadily onward to meet it. (See Matthew 16:21; 20:17–19.) Then, did He not suffer the most terrible kind of actual and physical pain when He was scourged, crowned with thorns, and crucified? (See Matthew 27:26, 29, 35.)

Because God spared not His own Son from the trials and sorrows of earth, God will not spare us similar experiences. After all, we are one in Christ. Yet being full of compassion and plenteous in mercy, God will see to it that the ill He does permit is for His glory and our present and eternal good. Did He not allow His children to be cast into the fiery furnace, thrown into the lion's den, and driven out from their homes to wander in sheepskins and goatskins? Yet God sanctified unto them these grievous trials and turned the curse into blessing. If He scourges with one hand, He supports with the other, and thus He is our consolation. (See Jeremiah 31:13.) As Bishop Handley Moule puts it,

> This heavy thing, it is His gift,
> His portion, thee is bless;
> Give it Him back; what shall He lift,
> No more on thee shall press.

No matter how fierce the fiery trial we are called upon to endure may be, our unfailing source of comfort is that we are journeying on to a sorrowless world, where there will be *"no more death, neither sorrow, nor crying, neither shall there be any more pain: for the former things are passed away"* (Revelation 21:4).

"Some Time We'll Understand"

Not now, but in the coming years,
It may be in the better land,
We'll read the meaning of our tears,
And there, some time, we'll understand.

We'll catch the broken thread again,
And finish what we here began;
Heav'n will the mysteries explain,
And then, ah, then, we'll understand.

We'll know why clouds instead of sun
Were over many a cherished plan;
Why song has ceased when scarce begun;
'Tis there, some time, we'll understand.

God knows the way, He holds the key,
He guides us with unerring hand;
Sometime with tearless eyes we'll see;
Yes, there, up there, we'll understand.

Then trust in God through all thy days;
Fear not, for He doth hold thy hand.
Though dark thy way, still sing and praise,
Some time, some time, we'll understand.
—*Maxwell N. Cornelius*

16

COMFORT IN COMFORTING OTHERS

"And there were also with him other little ships."
—Mark 4:36

After the death of Prince Albert, the heart of Queen Victoria the Good was crushed with grief. The days following were full of unspeakable sadness. The queen, however, was not so wrapped up in her own grief as not to feel the sorrows of others. Her first public words after the prince's death formed an expression of the most tender sympathy, sent to the wives and children of some two hundred men who were killed in the Hartley Colliery coal disaster of 1862. Thus a queen learned that there were *"other little ships."*

Further, Mark would have us consider the advantages of thinking of others. The consciousness of those other little ships out upon the same sea would have lessened the disciples' sense of need and reduced the weight of their own distress. Their cry for deliverance would not have been so selfish if they had considered others battling against the same storm. Thinking of others is always a help to ourselves. Whenever we think of our own trouble to the exclusion of the grief of others, our burden is magnified and our cross seems ten times heavier than it really is.

INSPIRES UNSELFISHNESS

Instead of centering all the pity and compassion of others upon ourselves, we think of our neighbors who deserve a share of the fellow feeling that makes us wondrous kind. We are not perfect until, saved from self-pity, we find joy in thinking of others. Alas! We can be guilty of selfishness even in the tears we shed and in the trials we bear.

BRINGS ENRICHMENT AND COMFORT

When we sink our personal grief in the consciousness of other suffering hearts, we not only help them bear their burdens but also take the sharp sting out of our own bitter experience. Thinking of others produces sacrifices whereby fellow sufferers are enriched. Thus our grief ennobles our own life and enriches others.

Do you think your life is of no account? Are you sometimes depressed by the obscurity of your sphere? Well, let Christ into your ship. Make Him the Pilot of your craft. Allow Him to calm your troubled conscience and settle your fear. Then, with steady helm and even keel, go out upon the tempest-driven sea and determine to lead some other little ship into the haven of peace. If you make this work your passion, what is left of life will take on a different hue, and you will come to the end of your days realizing that you have not lived in vain.

Remember, too, that God often permits personal trials not merely for the development of our own characters, but that our sorrows might make us a blessing to others who have similar trials. Often we meet Christ in the storms of life. In despair, we cry out for peace of heart and solace of mind, only to go out and discover other wave-beaten ships whose needs are just as great.

EMULATES THE DIVINE EXAMPLE

Jesus Christ was ever thinking of others. The thought of others was His life's passion and constant incentive; their dire need forced Him out of heaven into a sinful world. He flung His own life away in order that He might save others. While Jesus was on the cross, the chief priests mocked Him, saying, "*He saved others; himself he cannot save*" (Matthew 27:42). Make no mistake, Jesus could have saved Himself, but because He thought of others, He chose to stay on the cross. Oh, what self-forgetfulness is here portrayed! After two thousand years of soul-saving work, there are still others whom He must reach. Let us help the Savior to rescue other tempest-driven ships!

It is Mark alone who records the fact that those other little ships were "with Jesus." Anxious to get nearer to Christ and to have a more favorable position from which they might listen to His discourse, the onlookers probably took to their boats and followed Him. Thus, quickly, a little fleet gathered around Jesus.

Yet the disciples enjoyed a privilege of which the other little ships were deprived. It was into their ship the Master entered and in which He slept and from which He performed His miracle. Still, if other ships were denied His Person, they all participated in His peace and power. Being all around the sacred One, they shared in the tranquility which He made possible. When He stilled the storm and calmed the sea, He did so not merely for His disciples, but for all the storm-tossed vessels around.

Christ was in human form when this miracle was performed, and He could not, therefore, be in more than one place at a time. Now, however, by His Spirit, He can fill every life willing to give Him room. The miracle that evening was not for one ship but for all. In like manner, the divine provision of the cross is for all. Grace knows no favoritism. All Christ has of pardon, peace, and power is for all. All for all!

So, my reader, if Jesus is the Master of your boat, He yearns to be the Pilot of every other vessel. He wants you to help Him realize this plan. If through the billows of temptation, sorrow, disappointment, and death, you have found the miracle-working Lord and have entered into the secret of comfort, do not keep the treasure to yourself. Remember others! Do not be selfish with what you have and know of Christ, but take Him to others upon life's tempestuous sea. Finding other little ships about to sink, say to them, as they battle against troublous circumstances, "Friend, give Jesus the helm! Make Him the pilot of your life!" Then it will be true of others, even as it was of you, *"He calms the storm, so that its waves are still"* (Psalm 107:29). Then, *"well done, good and faithful servant"* (Matthew 25:21), will be His words of commendation and comfort for you.

At some moment I did answer Yes to Someone—or Something—and from that hour I was certain that existence is meaningful and that, therefore, my life in self-surrender, had a goal. From that moment I have known what it means "not to look back" and "to take no thought for the morrow."

—*Dag Hammarskjold*

PART III

COMFORT IN THE LAST THINGS

17

COMFORT WHEN CHRIST RETURNS

"When you hear of wars and revolutions, do not be frightened.
These things must happen first, but the end will not come right
away.' Then He said to them: 'Nation will rise against nation, and
kingdom against kingdom. There will be great earthquakes, famines
and pestilences in various places, and fearful events and great signs
from heaven. But before all this, they will lay hands on you and
persecute you. They will deliver you to synagogues and prisons, and
you will be brought before kings and governors, and all on account
of my name. This will result in your being witnesses to them. But
make up your mind not to worry beforehand how you will defend
yourselves. For I will give you words and wisdom that none of your
adversaries will be able to resist or contradict....All men will hate
you because of me. But not a hair of your head will perish.'"
—Luke 21:9–15, 17–18 (NIV)

Ours are ominous days! One hardly knows what is to happen next. International affairs change with startling rapidity. Somehow the world has lost its equilibrium, and politics and trade are topsy-turvy. Can it be we are living in the closing period of this wonderful age? Is it possible that every Christian will be removed out of the present chaotic condition of things before another sunrise? Is there any conspicuous sign heralding the imminent coming of the Lord? Are we on the threshold of the last great battle so clearly prophesied in God's divine program of coming events?

My own prayerful study of God's Word leads me to believe the church will not pass through the period known as "the tribulation." In the mercy of God, the church is to be delivered from its horrors. Nevertheless, it does seem as if the church is to witness the preparation for this tribulation. "Coming events cast their shadows before" them (Thomas Campbell). Walking in the shadows we may be, but the substance will never be ours if we are covered by the blood of the Lord Jesus Christ. What a blessed consolation is such a fact and faith!

Let us give ourselves, then, to the tracing of one of these conspicuous shadows. One notable feature of the change will be a remarkable unanimity, federation, and combination in all realms of life. A state of civilization is coming in which there will be no such thing as division. Perfect unity will prevail. The slogan will be amalgamation or annihilation! There is to be a world corporation. Controlling forces are to have *"one mind"* and are *"to agree"* (Revelation 17:13–17).

H. F. Welston remarked, "In the Scriptures, especially in Daniel and the Revelation, we are told that the culmination of the age is to be in a universal confederation of all the world's great schemes—national, political, commercial, social, and religious—under one head, to be administered by one great man, who will himself be under the guidance and support of the prince of this world. Toward this consummation, the wise have long seen that all the great world movements have been steadily tending as if by the guiding hand of some unseen power, working out a far-reaching and thoroughly-formed plan."

The "world corporation, born of industrial science and destined to combine education, industry, and government throughout the world in one system, will bring all nations and all peoples into *one complete body,* possessing one corporate mind." Such a "world corporation will displace all governments; nations will be helpless in its grasp; absorbing, controlling and eventually directing all phases of life, it will tear down the barriers of caste and nationality, and combine in one brotherhood all the people of earth, for one common purpose."

There are misguided thinkers who claim the inauguration of such a worldwide scheme will cure the ills of man's estate and bless the world with abiding peace. Man himself will rejoice in it, seeing that he ever glories in his power of achievement. Facing such a "world corporation" at the opening of the World Economic Conference many years ago, the chairman remarked, "And *you* can do it!" as he noted the ways the gathered statesmen could rectify the world's troubles.

World corporation, produced by man's effort, is sure to come. At the end of the age of a man, the man of sin, will combine and dominate all governments, commerce, industry, society, and apostate religion. This man will be filled with the pride of his own doings.

This fascinating utopia, however, instead of ushering in universal peace, will throw the world into a state of unparalleled tribulation and remorse. (See Matthew 24:21; Revelation 7:14.) It will be man's last futile attempt to govern the world, and will be brought to a speedy end by the coming of another Man, even the Son of Man from heaven, in power and glory to destroy the world corporation and its head and to introduce His own administration as the Prince of Peace.

There are three realms in which the man of sin is to hold sway: commerce, politics, and religion. As we examine these three realms, we will explore whether the foundation of such a corporation is presently being laid.

THE COMMERCIAL WORLD

No matter where we turn today, we find ourselves confronted with a craving for huge combines and trusts. The business world is fast shaping up for the time when the Beast will have full control of all aspects of commerce. There are gigantic trusts rapidly placing the capital and industries of the world into the hands of a few men, men that regulate for their own profit. Banks, industries, and products of all kinds are being swept into the hands of wealthy syndicates.

Individual interest is being eliminated. Private ownership, with all its concern for the worker, is becoming a thing of the past. Untold numbers of small firms are going out of business. Unless smaller firms and companies enter their own particular combine, they are more or less forced to cease trading, seeing that the great items of commerce are owned by great limited liability concerns, whose controlling shares are opening up the way for a sinister world ownership.

It is also an age of mechanical mass production. Everything is being standardized. Such a state of things is to flourish when all private concern is to cease and all commerce is to be brought under one controlling head and hand. The picture of this period has been sketched for us in the following words:

> *No man might buy or sell, save he that had the mark, or the name of the beast, or the number of his name.*   (Revelation 13:17)

There is to be the establishment of a universal boycott. Sitting at a table in some great center of the world, magnates and microphones in front of him, the Beast, with his mastermind, will control and command the whole earth. Dr. R. Middleton described how easily this could be initiated.

> With wondrous facilities for making his wishes known, he could grip each nation, each community, and each individual with his coils in an incredibly short space of time. His commands, sent through the press associations to every capital of the world, would quickly appear in special editions of the newspapers, and within a few brief hours, the whole world would not only know his will, but lie helplessly, unable to resist it.

The amalgamation of all trade centers under one head is gradually being realized. "The process of consolidation goes steadily on," said Philip Mauro, "and its inevitable end, if not interrupted, must obviously be the formation of a single, all-embracing monopoly."

By means of powerful combines and gigantic trusts, commerce is gathering rapidly into such iron-bound federations that the sources, both of supply and distribution, will become fewer and fewer. What a shrewd observer said of the United States of America can be applied to the realm of commerce: "The logical end must be that every industry will finally be owned and controlled by One Huge Trust."

Says Walter Scott, whose commentary on the *Revelation* is unsurpassed,

> Out of the seething masses of democracy, out of the wild forces of revolution and of anarchy which knows no law, out of the struggles and conflicts between capital and labor, out of the crushing of crowns and overturning of kingdoms, a strong and imperial power will emerge by direct satanic influences, and will crush all that is standing in its way, or bar its progress, and to this power, all without exception, must submit, or pay the penalty—death.   —*The Political World*

As we look out upon the political world of today, we cannot help but detect the selfsame craving for amalgamation. Playing at a game of grab, the nations speak about annexes, alliances, or the submergence of smaller nations. The map of the world is continually changing, and such reshuffling will continue until the confederacy of kings is reached, as indicated in Revelation 17:13–14 (NIV), "*They have one purpose and will give their power and authority to the beast. They will wage war against the Lamb, but the Lamb will overcome them.*"

"Several years ago," says an American writer, "dreams of colonial empires were prevalent and popular; today no statesman dare breathe the idea. Instead, he talks of autonomy, self-expression, a commonwealth of nations, a United States of Europe, and a federal government of the world, with all the nations related to one another somewhat as the states of the American republic and all working together to prevent world disaster."

In municipal life, also, we find a constant redistribution of area taking place. Villages and small towns have to surrender their long-prided independence. They must rest content with submergence into larger towns or cities. On a larger scale, Mussolini in Italy and Hitler in Germany have shown us how swiftly a nation can be unified and centralized in one person or order of things.

The United Nations assembly in New York, with all the peace pacts it has made, is clearly paving the way for the combination of these world powers referred to in Revelation 17:13–14. To return to Walter

Scott, that sane expositor of the powers in mind and action, "Note the distinction, 'their hearts' and 'his mind.'" Heartily they enter the work of destruction, but after all, they unknowingly accomplish the set purpose of God. The heart and mind of the destroying powers are united. They love the services to which, while they know it not, they have been divinely set apart, and they execute them with fixed determination.

God works unseen, but all the political changes of the day are in God's plan. The astute politicians and the clever diplomat are simply agents in the Lord's hands. Self-will and motives of policy may influence to action, but God is steadily working toward the end—the heavenly and earthly glory of His Son, the exaltation of the Lord Jesus. Thus, instead of kings and statesmen thwarting God's purpose, they are unconsciously forwarding it.

The climax and the perfection of world dominion, however, will be reached when the King of Kings returns to make the kingdoms of this world His own world-kingdom. The RV rightly substitutes *"the kingdom"* for *"the kingdoms"* (Revelation 11:15). To drop an *"s"* may seem to make a trivial difference, but *"kingdoms"* suggest many kings, numerous conflicting interests, and international jealousies. To contrast, the kingdom of the world (or world-kingdom) of our Lord and His Christ to come intimates one universal kingdom covering the globe, all parts of the earth being brought into subjection to the One reigning monarch. The government of the earth will be exercised by Jesus who will control all evil and establish all righteousness. His beneficent sway will be in every respect in happy contrast to past and present kingly rule and government. One undivided and universal kingdom covering the whole earth, and righteously and graciously governed, is the thought intended.

At present we live in the world of changing dynasties and falling monarchies. The constitutional changes of many countries are, to say the least, remarkable. Amid all the upheavals of national and international life, we hear a divine voice saying,

I will overturn, overturn, overturn, it...until he come whose right it is; and I will give it him.   (Ezekiel 21:27)

I will shake all nations, and the desire of all nations shall come.

(Haggai 2:7)

THE RELIGIOUS WORLD

Among the varying sects in Christendom, union is the foremost topic in conference discussion. Church leaders are thrilled with the prospect of one universal church. Barriers and theological differences dividing religious people must be broken down, and the way opened for a united religious organization. Advocates of church union affirm such a splendid ideal will not only eliminate all sectional strife and jealousy, but present a united front to the world.

Everything in the realm of religion appears to be working toward centralization and declension. Make no mistake about it; the unification of all religious denominations is coming. In the Roman Empire there will be the emergence of one universal church.

With the rapid development of science, television, computers, and the Internet in our own day, the organizations of the world, coupled with the latest scientific discoveries, are making it possible for one great mastermind to rule and command the world.

Beloved, we live in awesome days! With our fingers upon the world's pulse, are we not guilty of treachery if we keep back the truth regarding its perilous condition and future? Convert the world in the intervening short period, we cannot. Evangelize it, we must! May God help each of us, then, to make the most of these days of opportunity! A world of souls, and souls in the world need the Savior, and our supreme task is to present Him in all the fullness of His saving grace.

Lord, lay some soul upon my heart
And win that soul through me
And may I humbly do my part
To bring that soul to thee.
—*Unknown*

18

COMFORT IN THE GOLDEN YEARS

*"Moses was a hundred and twenty years old when he died,
yet his eyes were not weak nor his strength gone."*
—Deuteronomy 34:7 (NIV)

*"Even to your old age and gray hairs I am he, I am he who will
sustain you. I have made you and I will carry you."*
—Isaiah 46:4 (NIV)

*"Do not cast me away when I am old;
do not forsake me when my strength is gone."*
—Psalm 71:9 (NIV)

*"My eyes fail, looking for your promise; I say,
'when will you comfort me?'"*
—Psalm 119:82 (NIV)

The Bible has some precious promises for those who have reached the sunset years of life. Eliphaz, in one of his discourses with Job, combines *"the consolations of God"* with *"the grayheaded and very aged man"* (Job 15:10–11).

If there is one section of society in more need of divine comfort and cheer than another, it surely must be the seniors, many of whom are lonely and forgotten. Those who are parents are ever grateful to God if they have children who are loyal to them in their old age, "*a nourisher of thine old age*" (Ruth 4:15). As for the old themselves, if "*planted in the house of the* Lord," grace can be theirs to "*bring forth fruit*" to the glory of God "*in old age*" (Psalm 92:13–14). How apt are the lines of Robert Browning in "Rabbi Ben Ezra."

> Grow old along with me!
> The best is yet to be,
> The last of life, for which the first was made;
> Our times are in His hand,
> Who saith, "A whole I planned,
> Youth shows but half trust God; see all, nor be afraid!"

In the Old Testament, advancing age is described in varying ways. An old man is spoken of as "*grayheaded*" (1 Samuel 12:2) or "hoary-headed." (See Isaiah 46:4.) This latter term apparently implies a greater age than the former one. Job's very old age indicates a sign of withering strength. (See Job 15:10.) Respect is to be shown to the old (see Leviticus 19:32; Proverbs 23:22), and the decay of reverence for the aged is an evil omen. (See Deuteronomy 28:50; Isaiah 47:6.) It was proverbial to associate wisdom with the old whose experience qualified them for positions of trust and authority, hence, the terms "ancients" or "*elders*" as applied titles (Exodus 3:16; Acts 11:30). Yet there were exceptions to this recognition. (See Job 32:9; Psalm 119:100.)

Chapter 5 of Genesis is one of the most significant chapters when investigating the biblical aspect of longevity. Because it is filled with ancient Hebrew names, it appears to be laborious and is usually passed over as being unworthy of serious thought. Yet these names deserve study. As with all the names in the Bible, they are "fragments of ancient history, revelations of divine purposes, expressions of the hopes, the joys, the comforts, as well as the sorrows of the tried and tempted of those like ourselves, and prophecies that have been, or that are to be, fulfilled."

Genesis 5 spans the whole period from the creation of Adam to the days of Noah (a period of more than one thousand years), and it is a remarkable and instructive register of births and deaths. Along with the names of these earliest patriarchs, we have an account of how long each of them lived upon the earth. Adding up the years each one lived, we find that their united lives cover a period of 8,675 years. Enoch, who lived for the shortest period and who never died, was 365 years old before he was translated. God simply took him home as they were out walking together.

The longest-lived man in human history was Methuselah, who was 969 years old when he died, just 31 years short of a millennium! Noah, the grandson of Methuselah, lived for 950 years, but none of his contemporaries attained anything like that age. The degeneracy that brought the flood resulted in the shortening of the period which men were permitted to live upon the earth. Thus, between four and five hundred years after Noah's time, Abraham died at the age of 175. Although Moses dies at 120, he prescribed the ordinary limit of man's life as seventy years. (See Psalm 90:10; 103:14–16; Proverbs 10:27.) The witness of human history is that sin often shortens life. In our age, we may not live as long as those of old, yet we can comfort ourselves by remembering it is not the length of life that counts, but the quality of it.

The progress of civilization has not resulted in the lengthening of man's existence or in the enhancement of his enjoyment of life. In our time, departure from the simple life has resulted in unhealthy luxury. The average life span would be considerably increased by a return to a simple and more natural way of living. The presence of moral evil also tends to shorten life. The wonderful longevity recorded by Moses in Genesis 5 serves one very useful purpose, as Henry Thorne in his great work on Genesis pointed out.

> Such longevity made it possible for men to receive the traditions of the Creation and of the Fall, during a period of many centuries, from one who had lived before the Fall, and from others who were born at periods not very remote from that of that sad catastrophe. It is possible that Adam lived for about 113 years

after the birth of Methuselah, and Methuselah cannot have been more than 369 years old when his grandson Noah was born. There can be very little room for doubt, therefore, if we accept the chronology of this chapter we are considering that Noah conversed with one who had conversed with Adam, and that Enoch himself had the privilege of conversing with Adam himself. God knows how to preserve His truth for the guidance and sanctification of His creatures, though the ungodly turn away from it and do their utmost to pervert it. The genealogy of this chapter is, like all other portions of the Bible, a finger post that directs attention to the messiah. The generation of Adam, as given here, is part of the generation of the Second Adam, Luke 3:23–28, and it is for this reason that it is so minutely described and so carefully preserved. Let us be thankful for everything God has told us concerning Him Who is the only Savior of men.

Having considered the significance of the most aged mentioned in sacred history, let us dwell for a little upon the attitude of the God of all comfort toward the aging and the aged of our own times. First of all, the question arises as to when, in the course of life, we become old or aged. In Great Britain and the United States, when people reach sixty-five years of age they become entitled to the old age pension (or Social Security). For those who have worked in firms or factories, this usually means the cessation of their position. Yet in many cases, these persons at sixty-five are healthier than their counterparts of some fifty years ago, and although forced to retire because of pensionable age, they are still capable of working effectively.

A comparatively modern area of medical science known as gerontology provides a study of the phenomena of aging. It is represented as a progressive inability to cope with environmental demands and is reflected in an increasing probability of death as individuals age. Yet at the age of one hundred and twenty, Moses found his strength unabated, implying he could have lived on, had it been the divine will that he should lead the people he had brought from Egypt into the Promised

Land. Gerontology, however, is more taken up with the aging process, seeking to discover how the disabilities and handicaps of old age can be minimized rather than trying to extend the life span. Geriatrics, on the other hand, is the branch of medical science concerned with the prevention and treatment of diseases in older people.

Life potential may vary according to environmental, economic, or hereditary factors, but few, in comparison, reach the one hundred year span. Very few indeed live beyond the one hundred year mark. It is believed there is a gradual reduction of the performance of the organic system beginning at thirty to thirty-five years of age. The system declines through life thereafter. There are, of course, individual differences. Some at seventy possess the performance expectancy of the average fifty-year-old. There is a maximum age beyond which an individual cannot live, even under the most favorable conditions. As Christians, we believe the duration of one's life is a secret known only to God who is declared to be *"the length of your days"* (Deuteronomy 30:20 NKJV). He has our times in His hands and offers Himself to be our *"guide even unto death"* (Psalm 48:14).

Older men and women must behave in a holy manner if they are to experience the full blessing of the promise, *"Even to hoar hairs will I carry you"* (Isaiah 46:4; See also Titus 2:2–5). The Lord has precious consolation for those who grow old in His service. Anna, who had been a widow for eighty-four years, *"served God with fastings and prayers night and day"* as she *"looked for redemption in Jerusalem"* (Luke 2:37–38). If she married at twenty, as was probable, she must have been over one hundred when great comfort came to her at the glorious news of the Savior's birth. She instantly gave thanks. (See Luke 2:36–38.)

Most earnestly David prayed, *"Now also when I am old and grey-headed, O God, forsake me not; until I have showed thy strength unto this generation, and thy power to every one that is to come"* (Psalm 71:18). Previously, however, he pled with God, *"Cast me not off in the time of old age; forsake me not when my strength faileth"* (Psalm 71:9).

The comfort of those who are older is that although heart and flesh may fail, God will not forsake. He will carry them in His everlasting arms until He determines the day of their entrance into His presence and glory. Right on through the evening of old age, God has promised to supply our every need, to comfort us with His love, to relieve us with His mercy, to defend us with His justice, and to make us eternally secure by His covenant. For the saint, the best is yet to be for believing in Him, they *"shall never die"* (John 11:26). Thus, when death comes and *"the silver cord is severed"* (Ecclesiastes 12:6 NIV), it will be as a friend not as a foe, even if the death tragic. (See Matthew 10:28.)

> I am serene because I know thou lovest me.
> Because thou lovest me,
> naught can move me from my peace.
> Because thou lovest me,
> I am as one to whom all good has come.
> —Translated from Gaelic by *Alistair MacLean*

19

COMFORT IN THE VALLEY OF SHADOWS

"Yea, though I walk through the valley of the shadow of death, I will fear no evil; for You are with me; Your rod and Your staff, they comfort me."
—Psalm 23:4 (NKJV)

"As a mother comforts her child, so will I comfort you."
—Isaiah 66:13 (NIV)

"'Lazarus is dead.'...Jesus wept."
—John 11:14, 35 (NIV)

"Do not let your hearts be troubled. Trust in God; trust also in me. In my Father's house are many rooms; if that were not so, I would have told you. I am going there to prepare a place for you. And if I go and prepare a place for you, I will come back and take you to be with me that you also may be where I am. You know the way to the place where I am going."
—John 14:1–4 (NIV)

*"Now we know that if the earthly tent we live in is destroyed, we
have a building from God, an eternal house in heaven, not built by
human hands. Now it is God who has made us for this very purpose and has given us the Spirit as a deposit, guaranteeing what is
to come. Therefore we are always confident and know that as long
as we are at home in the body we are away from the Lord."*
—2 Corinthians 5:1, 5–6 (NIV)

Augustine W. Hare died in 1834. In his volume, *Guesses at Truth*, he
wrote, "The ancients dreaded death; the Christian can only fear dying."
Yet Hare was mistaken, for the Bible reveals that many of the ancients
did not dread death. Rather, they looked upon death as being precious
in God's sight. Through grace, they could sing, "The fear of death has
gone forever." Charles Kingsley was so perplexed over insoluble problems that he exclaimed, "O Death, Sweet Death, when wilt thou come
and tell me all I want to know?"

Death to the believer is not a final end, but the opening of the door
into a richer, more abundant, and unending life. When we pass from
time into eternity, sublime consolation will be ours, if we welcome death
as a friend and not a foe. How impressive are the lines of that renowned
poet, Walt Whitman, who died in 1892.

Come lovely and soothing death,
Undulate round the world, serenely arriving, arriving,
In the day, in the night, to all, to each,
Sooner or later, delicate death.
Prais'd be the fathomless universe,
For life and joy, and for objects and knowledge curious,
And for love, sweet love—but praise! Praise! Praise!
For the sure-enwinding arms of cool-enfolding death.

In our present day the ideals of life have become more secular,
making a meditation such as this more imperative. Men are liable
to focus their thoughts upon the world that now is. Goethe has said

somewhere, "We may well leave the next world to reveal itself to us in due time, since we shall soon enough be there and know all about it. Leave the next world to reveal itself in due time!" It sounds eminently sensible and wise, but it fails entirely to reckon with the human heart. When all goes well and prosperity smiles upon us, it may be easy to dismiss the thought of eternity from our minds, but when our homes are emptied or the golden gate into paradise begins to open for our own entrance, it is useless to tell us not to be concerned about death and destiny.

Thus the practical secularism of our day, producing as it does the danger of a "steady ebb from the shores of another life," has caused the fading of what John Ruskin called the "heaven light" out of the life of the average person. Our vision has become limited to the cares and duties and pleasures of this passing day. We must remind our hearts that our existence here is but initial.

The Jews have a saying, "In this life, death never suffers a man to be glad." This is so, for death is always a tragedy to someone. Never a day passes without death breaking some heart. Never a corner is safe from the dripping rain of death's tears. Death is the skeleton at every feast, the bitterness in every cup, the discord in our music. It is the nameless dread that has haunted man from the time when grief was first born in a mother's broken heart, as Eve knelt by the side of her boy murdered by the passionate violence of his own brother. Death has not lost its fearful countenance. It is still a tremendous and terrible fact all of us have to meet. Ignore it we cannot, since it is continually intruding into the circle of our loved ones and acquaintances.

Hamlet's great soliloquy still overwhelms many with its fear of death and the life beyond.

> To die, to sleep—
> To sleep, perchance to dream—ay, there's the rub,
> For in that sleep of death what dreams may come,
> When we have shuffled off this mortal coil,
> Must give us pause;

...The dread of something after death,
The undiscover'd country, from whose bourn
No traveler returns, puzzles the will,
And makes us rather bear those ills we have,
Than fly to others that we know not of?
(3.1.63–67, 77–81)

DEATH IS INEVITABLE

The fact of death or physical dissolution is the inevitable lot of all mankind. One writer has a terse way of stating this truth,

Certain things may be done by proxy, other things may be bought off and evaded; but we cannot evade death. Each man and woman, saint and scoundrel alike, passes through the portal of the tomb. Life, in some respects, is like a game of chess. Upon the board, during the progress of the game, the pieces occupy different positions and possess different values; but when the game is over, all alike, bishops, kings, knights, and pawns, go into the common box. In life here below, one man is a king, another is a bishop, another is the master of a great business, another is a menial, a mere pawn. But when death comes—the great leveler—all men are equal in the solemn stillness of the sepulcher.

DEATH IS UNCERTAIN

Although the fact of death is certain, yet the day or the hour of its coming no one knows. At times, sickness or natural decay gives notice of its approach, but the exact moment of the "lifting of the curtain upon the unseen" is hidden. Because it is the one experience overtaking the entire human race, it behooves us to set our house in order and to pray,

Teach me to live that I may dread
The grave as little as my bed;
Teach me to die, that so I may
Rise glorious at that awful day.
—*Author Unknown*

DEATH IS TERMINATION

Of course death is not the termination of our existence. It is not a *state*, but an *act*; it is not an abode in which we dwell, but a gate we pass through into a richer, fuller life. Because the "substance of the soul is indissoluble, and therefore indestructible," as Bishop Handley Moule pointed out in His *Outlines of Christian Doctrine*, the mysterious "I" can never terminate. Moral personality is mysteriously permanent, as God has constituted things. Moule also noted that death is the end of many things we cherish, such as:

Our physical beauty, for the fairest form is made revolting by the power of death.

Our material riches, for no matter what possessions we may accumulate, we must leave the world as naked as we entered it. Alexander was buried with his open hands outside his coffin, indicating that he left the world as empty as he came into it. When one dies, we hear it said: "How much did he leave?" How much? Why, he left it all, for nothing can be carried on but one's character.

Our earthly honors, whether religious, social, scholastic, or national, all vanish like faded leaves, when death removes us from both the praise and blame of man. The only honor we carry with us is that of a life lived nobly and well in Christ's great cause.

DEATH IS NECESSARY

We should not look upon death with horror, as if it were altogether a monster or a robber, snatching from us all that we may cling to in life. Death is a necessary law of nature to which we must submit. It is an event, not a catastrophe; a stopping place on our journey; a slowing down as we come into the station, not a terminus.

If people never died, the world would become too crowded to be habitable. E. C. Spurr stated in *Death and the Hereafter*, "People speak of death as if it were something horrible and to be afraid of. But life should be regarded socially as a banquet to which many guests are invited, and where there are many sittings. The first take their place, and, having finished, make way for other relays, until all are served. If we were here forever, the first-comers to the banquet would gain all; the last-comers nothing."

DEATH IS GAIN

Death works no magic, produces no change, and performs no miracle for the dying one. Yet many seem to feel that all they have to do when they come to die is to solicit the ministrations of parsons or priests, as if they had power to make them die and wake up saints. The mere act of transferring from one house to another in no way changes the person removing. We continue on the other side as we depart from this side, for good or bad. This life determines that fact.

The solemn thing, then, is to live well, and thus solve in advance the mystery of death. We must lift from death the power to betray us. If we can say, *"For to me to live is Christ,"* then, when we come to pull up the tent pegs and roll up the canvas, dying grace will be ours to say with supreme confidence, *"To die is gain"* (Philippians 1:21 NIV).

The date is fixed on which we must look death in the face. There is a spot marked where our dust must return to its natural abode, where the world's ambitions, the strife of tongues, and conflicts of passions will float past but as evening winds sighing over a deserted shrine.

Queen Elizabeth I is said to have cried out at the end of her life, "All my possessions for a moment of time!" but there was no one to barter with her. If our lives are lived in the light of eternity, when we hear the divine voice saying, "Come up higher," we shall not crave for a further moment of time for death will be a birth. As the eyes of the baby open upon the sunlight of earth when the tiny mass of humanity leaves the darkness of the womb, so when we close our eyes in the darkness of

death we will open them on a "light that never was on sea or land."
(Wordsworth)

This, then, is our consolation: absent from the body, we shall be at
home with the Lord. The hymnist H. F. Lyte taught us to sing,

> I fear no foe with Thee at hand to bless;
> Ills have no weight, and tears no bitterness;
> Where is death's sting? Where, grave, thy victory?
> I triumph still, if Thou abide with me.
>
> Reveal Thyself before my closing eyes;
> Shine through the gloom, and point me to the skies;
> Heaven's morning breaks, and earth's vain shadows flee;
> In life, in death, O Lord, abide with me.

20

COMFORT IN HEAVEN

True, human life is exhilarating and there is so much discovery and romantic adventure here and now, so why be concerned about a distant hereafter? When a dear one crosses the barrier and heart and home are left vacant, then we pause to think on where we are going rather than where we are, and interest is awakened in what has happened to the one "we loved and lost awhile." Many questions clamor for an answer. Where has our beloved one gone? What is he or she doing? Can the precious dead see and hear us? Are consciousness and memory retained? The question George MacDonald asked is one we all ask when we face the overwhelming experience of loss and sorrow:

> Traveler, what lies over the hill?
> Traveler, tell to me;
> I am only a child—from the window-sill,
> Over I cannot see.

Too often, however, the loneliness of parting passes, time covers the wound, and gradually we think less of the distant scene. Back to the present we come, with questions of a future life no longer uppermost and pressing for answers. Yet for true Christians, there should be the constant remembrance that we are only strangers and pilgrims in this world; that heaven is our home. The joy, the wonder, the exuberance of a never-ending life in the Savior's presence should always possess our minds, for in such a heavenly hope there is a blessed serenity. If heaven is ever in our hearts, then at death we will go bounding home as school-children do when classes and lessons are over, hastening home to dear ones awaiting our coming.

What is wrong with those of us who believe our citizenship is already in heaven? Where is the thrill, the wonder, the eager anticipation John expressed, when, as an old man of some ninety years of age, he was yet like an eager youth awaiting a glorious adventure when he exclaimed,

> *Dear friends, now we are children of God, and what we will be has not yet been made known. But we know that when he appears, we shall be like him, for we shall see him as he is. Everyone who has this hope in him purifies himself, just as he is pure.* (1 John 3:2 NIV)

A life with such a vision is emancipated from the dreary and monotonous feeling gripping many today. Outlook gives zest to life and enables us to cram earth with heaven. Living with our eyes on the far horizon does not make us indifferent to our present obligations. We do not become so heavenly-minded as to be of no earthly use. The joy set before us enables us to face life's trials with a calm resignation and inspires us to pack the very best into the little while between. As each day's work ends and we nightly pitch our tent, our hearts are elated with the glorious thought that it is another day's march nearer home and the days are not accumulating before us as they are behind us. Each one is less "a sunset nearer every night; a sunset nearer glory bright." ("A Little While," Ada R. Habershon, 1899)

Our prayer should be for a more constant contemplation of the blessed estate awaiting us, and of the country in which sickness, pain, sorrow, farewells, and death are unknown. How enthused we ought to be over such a land in which no eyes are ever wet with tears, and brows never have a shade or wrinkle, and limbs never tire in the service of the King! There, fear and dread are unknown, and the inhabitants "count not time by years, for there is no night there." ("No Night There," John R. Clements, 1899).

Danson Smith carried such a sentiment in the verse,

> There is no night of things unknown, uncertain;
> Things which now try the heart to make it strong.
> There is no night—there is no veiling curtain—
> Just light, and bliss, and joy, and endless song.

Awaiting such a glorious consummation does not mean we will wait indolently. No, the scenes of a sweeter day will serve to wean our hearts from so much that is empty in the present changing world order and fix hem upon the heavenly and eternal. Dr. Graham Scroggie reminded us, "If this is one we shall live well here by living much there; we shall have a truer perspective, and worthier sense of values. We shall not mistake imitation gems for priceless jewels; nor shall we throw away eternal gains for momentary gains. To live well in this world we must be other-worldly. Time is our opportunity to prepare for Eternity, and this world is the sphere in which to qualify for the next." Dr. Billy Graham wrote,

> When my maternal grandmother died, for instance, the room seemed to fill with a heavenly light. She sat up in bed and almost laughingly said, "I see Jesus. He has His arms outstretched toward me. I see Ben (her husband who had died some years earlier) and I see the angels." She slumped over, absent from the body but present with the Lord. What a glorious experience for the believer!

As we view with wonder the place called heaven, our hearts are filled with comfort and joy. Like a golden thread, the glories of heaven are woven into the fabric of every book of the Bible. Our inquiring minds seek the answer to six questions relating to spiritual comfort.

+ Will we have friends in heaven?
+ Will we have children in heaven?
+ Will we be angels in heaven?

+ Will we have rewards in heaven?

+ Will we have joy in heaven?

+ Will there be evil and good in heaven?

FRIENDS IN HEAVEN

A friend asked George MacDonald, "Shall we know one another in heaven?" His pointed reply was, "Shall we be greater fools in paradise than we are here?" Consciousness, fellowship, love, memory, and personal identity involve recognition. Each individual, himself or herself here, will possess hereafter a recognizable personality and faculties superior to those exercised on earth. We may not have the full understanding of the *mode* of recognition in heaven, but of the *fact* there need be no doubt. Paul reminds us that heaven is the home of the *"whole family in heaven and earth"* (Ephesians 3:15). What kind of a home would it be if its members are to be strangers to each other forever? We can assume with certainty we shall know one another more thoroughly in the life beyond? *"Then shall I know even as also I am known"* (1 Corinthians 13:12). Heaven means a more holy, blessed intimacy, our present human frailties prevent.

Further, this age-long and passionate desire has a strong sentimental value and is likewise a perfectly legitimate one. Heaven would not be heaven if it did not offer reunion with, and the recognition of, our dead in Christ. All *"love is of God"* (1 John 4:7), John reminds us, and because love cannot be buried in a coffin, the beautiful but broken relationships of earth are resumed in the Father's home above where as members of the same family we dwell together in perfect harmony.

The Bible offers sufficient evidence of recognition among the occupants of heaven. We can be perfectly sure the angels round about the throne of God know one another. Associated in the same service of praising the Lord and carrying out divine behests, we must infer that these glorious spirits know each other. Surely, the two angels found sitting at the Savior's tomb and who announced His resurrection recognized one another!

Further, the Old Testament saints believed when they left earth, they would join their relatives in another world and resume fellowship with them. (See Genesis 25:8; 35:29; 49:33.) Believing Joseph was dead, "*Jacob tore his clothes, put on sackcloth and mourned for his son many days. All his sons and daughters came to comfort him, but he refused to be comforted. 'No' he said, 'in mourning will I go down to the grave to my son.' So his father wept for him*" (Genesis 37:34–35 NIV). Actually, Jacob meant that he would go sorrowfully into the other world, there to be joined together again with Joseph. Jesus spoke about sitting down with Abraham, Isaac, and Jacob in heaven. How could He do this without recognizing them? What kind of a fellowship could they be if these patriarchs have not retained their identity? (See Matthew 8:11.)

David, as he wept over his dead child, knew he would join him again in death: "*I shall go to him*" (2 Samuel 12:23). Remember, David had only seen the baby Bathsheba had borne him but a few days, yet he believed he would distinguish his son from the millions in heaven. David looked beyond the vast universe to the place of reunion, saying, "My child is there. I shall go to him." The value of such a hope is better understood as we remember that David, as a man after God's own heart, knew as much about the mind of God and the nature of the other world as almost any other Old Testament writer. Did not King Saul recognize Samuel when God permitted him to return for a few brief seconds to announce Saul's doom? (See 1 Samuel 28:14.)

Two men came down from heaven to have a conversation with Jesus about His death at Jerusalem. Jesus had taken three of His disciples, Peter, James, and John, to the summit of a mountain, and while there the two heavenly visitants appeared: Moses and Elijah. (See Matthew 17:1–8.) Peter, of course, had never seen these Old Testament saints in the flesh, yet he immediately recognized them, for he said, "Let us make three tabernacles, one for Moses, one for Elijah and one for Thee." Thus, their identity must have been unimpaired.

The rich man in hell recognized both Abraham and Lazarus. (See Luke 16:19–31.) While there is much mystery in the incident Jesus related, it is evident there was unmistakable recognition. Identity had not been destroyed. Our Lord also taught that memory is immortal in the next world, for Abraham said to Dives, *"Son, remember that thou in thy lifetime receivedst thy good things"* (Luke 16:25). In His resurrection body, Jesus retained His identity. In the twilight, Mary supposed Jesus to be the gardener. To all intents and appearance, He was a human being, and as soon as He spoke, Mary recognized the voice—the same voice that had previously spoken to her soul. The two disciples on the road to Emmaus did not recognize Jesus for the special reason Luke explains, *"Their eyes were holden that they should not know him"* (Luke 24:16). Later at supper, as He broke bread, the film fell from their eyes and they instantly recognized Him. *"They knew him"* (verse 31). Paul would not have desired to be with Christ if he had not been sure of recognizing Him again as the one he saw on that road to Damascus. (See Acts 9; Philippians 1:21.)

As to the righteous being able to converse with the Lord in heaven, if we can speak to Him now in prayer, surely we shall be able to do so more perfectly over there. How could we be "at home" with God and not recognize Him and be recognized by Him? Social fellowship, so far from ceasing in heaven, will be vastly extended, and each of us will know intuitively the whole family of God. What a gathering of the ransomed that will be! If you have a dear one in heaven your heart yearns to see, do not despair for you will meet again. The voice you loved to hear, you will hear again. The identity of the one you were near to on earth remains the same, and instant recognition will be yours as you meet never to part again. Your beloved one is only "lost awhile."

Not only will we meet our dear ones again, but we will meet the great saints of the ages, Abraham, Moses, David, Paul, and all the rest of the prophets and apostles as well as the martyrs and the worthies of the centuries. As we meet them on the golden streets above, we will be able to converse with them without restraint. As children of the same family and all in heaven through the grace of God, introductions will be unnecessary as we shall all meet on the common ground of relationship. The poet asked,

Shall we know the friends that greet us
In that glorious spirit land?
Shall we see the same eyes shining
On us as in the days of yore?
Shall we feel the dear arms turning
Fondly, round us as before?

John Henry Newman, in "Lead, Kindly Light" (1833), answered the question:

And with the morn those angel faces smile
Which I have loved long since and lost awhile.

If we accept the fact of recognition in the hereafter, then will all conventional relationships of this life to be continued in the life beyond? Do we carry over into the future state all the social associations of earth? The Sadducees sought an answer from Jesus about the relationship of the seven brothers married to the one woman, whom each man took as his wife as each one died. (See Mark 12:18–19.) Surely she could not have the seven husbands around her in heaven? Jesus answered,

> *Are you not in error because you do not know the Scriptures or the power of God? When the dead rise, they will neither marry nor be given in marriage; they will be like the angels in heaven. Now about the dead rising—have you not read in the book of Moses, in the account of the bush, how God said to him, "I am the God of Abraham, the God of Isaac, and the God of Jacob"? He is not the God of the dead, but of the living. You are badly mistaken!*
>
> (Mark 12:24–27 NIV)

Our glorified bodies will be so changed that in our new environment, present bodily needs and desires will be extinct. There is no propagation in heaven. Hunger will not be ours for the Lord in the midst of the throne is to feed us. Spiritual affinities are to make us one in heaven. All that is sensual in love is purged away. Ellicott comments,

The old relations may subsist under new conditions. Things that are incompatible here may there be found to co-exist. The saintly wife of two saintly husbands may love both with an angelic, and therefore a pure and unimpaired affection.

But while sexual relations end with this life, we have no reason for believing that all social relations do also. True love is eternal, and the objects of this love on earth will be loved in a purer way above where life reaches a perfect fulfillment.

Heaven is not a sphere of ethereal, implied, cold, unsocial, and formless spirits, but a home of saints with glorified bodies having a perpetual interchange of perfect love and affection. Graven on the tombstone marking the place where Charles Kingsley and his much-loved wife lie buried are the three Latin words: *Amavimus, Amamus, Amabimus*, meaning, "We have loved; we love; we shall love." Such was Kingsley's faith, and such is ours. Over there we shall continue to love; the only difference our love will be redeemed.

Inquiring hearts often want to know whether those in heaven can see and know what is happening to us—whether they are cognizant of life here below—and whether they take an interest in our lives and can pray for us. Expositors and commentators differ on such questions. The Bible nowhere clearly states that those in heaven can see us at all times. If they could, they could hardly refrain from sorrow and tears as they view the troubles and suffering of loved ones on earth. It may be that occasionally, by special dispensation, God allows those who have died to see those on earth, as in the case of the rich man and Lazarus, but aside from this account in Luke 16, there is little Scripture to support any contention that the dead have a continuing acquaintance with life on the earth.

A passage like that of being surrounded by *"a cloud of witnesses"* (Hebrews 12:1 NIV) has been used to suggest heaven is not closed to earth, and our warfare and welfare here below is still observed by those above; our race is being run in an arena surrounded by those who have passed on before as spectators still interested in our spiritual progress.

C. H. Spurgeon addressed this in an eloquent sermon in which he speaks in the gymnastic style taken from the Olympic exercises.

> With a wave of the hand the Apostle directs us to the spectators who throng the sides of the course. There were always such at those races: each city and state fielded its contingent, and the assembled throng watched with eager eyes the efforts of those who strove for the mastery. Those who look down upon us from yonder heavens are described as "so great a cloud of witnesses." These compass us about. Thousands upon thousands, who have run this race before, and have attained their crowns, behold us from their heavenly seats, and mark how we behave ourselves. This race is worth running, for the eyes of "the nations of them which are saved" are fixed upon us. This is not a hole-in-the-corner business, this running for the great prize. Angels and principalities, powers and hosts redeemed by blood, have mustered to behold the glorious spectacle of men agonizing for holiness and putting forth their utmost strength to copy the Lord Jesus. Ye that are men, now run for it! If there be any spiritual life and gracious strength in you, put it forth today; for patriarchs and prophets, saints, martyrs, and the apostles look down from heaven upon you.

We can imagine how those who listened to such descriptive preaching must have been carried away, but the fact remains that the narrative Spurgeon preached from does not say that those who have passed on are looking down on us from heaven, but simply that we are surrounded by a company of witnesses, namely, those heroes of faith mentioned in the previous chapter. Those worthies in Hebrews 11 lived lives testifying to the faith. The word *"witnesses"* does not and cannot mean spectators. The Greek word for witnesses used here is *martus* from which we have "martyr." These were men and women whose lives witnessed to the power of faith.

The argument has been advanced that the departed can know about us without enduring pain because of trials here below. Our Lord does not suffer pain of heart, even though He looks down upon the sin and anguish of earth. He sees the end from the beginning, and with His vision of a glorious consummation does not sorrow as others. Scripture, however, is silent on the question of heaven being cognizant of earth. It is best to follow the silence of the Scripture and await the future. This fact is certain: five minutes after death we shall have all the answers to our questions. At this point we can register our rejection of spiritualism or spiritism which teaches that the dead do know all about us and can come back and converse with us through spiritualistic mediums. While there may be a good deal of quackery associated with séances, yet all is not false. So-called messages from the dead, if not the deliberate skillful manipulation and deception of mediums, may be the efforts of evil spirits who are able to impersonate the dead. The dead cannot return to commune with us, but as one writer suggested, "There is no reason why our Lord may not be properly asked, in submission of course to His will, to convey messages to our holy dead."

> *Each one had a harp and they were holding golden bowls full of incense, which are the prayers of the saints. And they sang a new song.*   (Revelation 5:8–9 NIV)

Scripture, likewise, does not confirm the somewhat pleasing and sentimental assertion that our departed friends are silently and secretly with us, just as we have the spiritual presence of Christ, that loved ones are not separated from us in some far-off, closed-up heaven. Poet John Oxenham expresses the feelings of parents on learning that their son had died.

> He is gone...yet he is near us,
> Maybe he can see and hear us,
> Yes we feel him nearer, dearer,
> Tears have washed our souls' eyes clearer.

A similar sentiment of the nearness of our precious dead can be found in these further lines,

> Linger a little, invisible host
> Of the saved dead, who stand

Perhaps not far off,
Though men may scoff,
Touch me with unfelt hands.

CHILDREN IN HEAVEN

If they die before they reach the years of moral choice and the power to discern between right and wrong, children pass right into the presence of Jesus by virtue of His atoning work upon the cross. Original sin they do have, but that is covered by Christ's blood. Practiced sin they do not have and therefore are not guilty of transgressions incurring the wrath of God. As for the mentally deficient, they enter heaven upon the same conditions.

How came these children there,
Singing Glory, Glory, Glory?
Because the Savior shed His blood
To wash away their sin,
Bathed in that precious purple flood,
Behold them white and clean,
Singing Glory, Glory, Glory.

A matter perplexing the heart of many a Christian parent who has a baby in heaven is whether that little one will remain in the same state above. Do girls and boys have their purpose in heaven as such? A twin answer is offered for this question. First, there are those who feel that without children in heaven much would be missed by the godly parents who bore them; if we depart as child, youth or patriarch, so we remain. When Christ raises the body at His return, he will raise it as it was but withal glorified. Thus, a child of one year will still be, in size and appearance, a child a year old. A mother will have her child as a child forever. Preaching on the theme of recognition in heaven, Bishop Simpson broke out in his sermon with the question, "What would heaven be to me without my Willie?"—Willie being his dear son whom death had recently claimed.

The second approach is that growth and increase will be characteristic of children in heaven. Parents crossing the threshold of the life beyond will instantly discover that their child, or children, have grown to a glorified maturity. Under the creative touch of God and under the tutelage of their angel teachers they steadily grew into a perfect character. F. C. Spurr tells of a friend who had lost a child and sent him a silver printed card bearing these words,

> In memory of our little Donald,
> Lent to us for two years;
> The sunshine of our home,
> Recalled by the Father,
> Now at school with the angels for his tutors.

Such a hope is a comforting and satisfying one for those who believe that the lambs gathered to His bosom reach the full stature of glorified manhood or womanhood. Just what the exact future holds for the children who die before their innocence is lost, Scripture does not say. In this faith, however, we can rest that our dear ones are not lost to us, and that no matter what change may overtake them, they will still be ours. All the redeemed, like the angels, will possess endless youth, activity, power, knowledge, and holiness, and will experience the same immortal happiness, dignity, and divine favor. They will be lovely, beautiful, and glorious in the sight of God.

> My knowledge of that life is small,
> The eye of faith is dim;
> But 'tis enough that Christ knows all,
> And I shall be with Him.
> ("Lord, It Belongs Not to My Care," Richard Baxter, 1681)

ANGELS IN HEAVEN

An error that must be corrected is that children, or for that matter all the saints, are to be angels in heaven. That hymns are not always biblical is evident from the children's hymn with a verse that reads:

> I want to be an angel
> And with the angels stand;
> A crown upon my forehead,
> And harp within my hand.

Our Lord clearly taught we are to resemble the holy angels in some of their attributes, but never that we are to be angels. All the saints in heaven will be glorified human beings, as distinct from the angels as they are distinct from the Lord of glory. Neither are we to spend eternity "singing around the throne" with harp in hand. Song there will be, but also service, fitted to our individuality. As real beings, possessed of spiritual bodies and quickened intellects, we shall be active, serving the Lord as we cannot here below because of the trammeling influences of the flesh.

It is true that we are to rest from our labors, but the word for labor here means a *painful strain*—a feeling never experienced in heaven where eternal, untiring youth and strength will be ours in the carrying out of God's glorious commissions. In His temple there will be no long sermons and meaningless ritual, but a delightful and unceasing serving and rejoicing. Weariness and tedium will never be ours, only a constant, happy, and privileged activity. As Dr. Alexander Smellie so beautifully expressed it,

> God bring me to Jerusalem! God bring me home in peace! It is the heart's uttermost attained at length. It is the heart's harbor made after the stormy sea.
>
> There my senses will be marvelously transfigured and sublimed; so that I shall hunger no more and thirst no more, and I shall behold Christ's face, and I shall hear the songs of the seraphim.
>
> There my intellect will have its doubt resolved and its mysteries cleared, and I shall know even as also I am known.
>
> There my memory will cease to be haunted by grievous recollections of past sins; for I shall live in the presence of my Savior, and His grace will be all my thought.

There my conscience will have its alarms stilled and its perplexities made plain; it will see and follow Him Who has brought in for it a perfect righteousness.

There my will will never be visited by uprisings of rebellion and disobedience; Jesus will lead me in perpetual triumph behind His chariot-wheels.

There my affections will be satisfied. "I go," as Jacob Bohme said, "to be with my Redeemer and my King in Paradise."

O, sweet and blessed country!

Wise theologians of old divided the happiness of heaven into what they called the *essential* and *accidental* joys. By *essential*, they implied the satisfaction the soul derives immediately from God's presence and from the beatific vision.

> What rapture will it be
> Prostrate before Thy Throne to lie,
> And gaze and gaze on Thee.

The great and crowning truth about the heavenly life awaiting us is that it will be a life eternally lived in unspeakable glory. The disciples had a fleeting glimpse of that glory when, on the Mount of Transfiguration, they were eyewitnesses of the Lord's majesty. Ours will be the privilege of basking continually in the full blaze of that glory. Samuel Rutherford, that seraphic, covenanting preacher, fell into raptures whenever he thought of heaven.

Oh, how sweet and glorious shall our case be when that Fairest among the sons of men will lay His fair face to our sinful eyes and wipe away all tears from our eyes. O time, run swiftly, and hasten that day.

Similarly, we find Augustine expressing the same hope.

Christ shall be the end of all our longing and desire! Him shall we perpetually see! Him shall we love without tediousness and grief! And Him shall we praise without ending.

> Just to be near the dear Lord I adore,
> That will be glory—be glory for me.

By *accidental*, the old divines implied those additional joys coming from reunion with loved ones and friends, meeting the saints of all ages, joyous occupations, and all the delights of ever-widening knowledge. A multitude of secondary joys will spring from the many surprises heaven holds for us. Christians will be there we hoped to meet, and some will be there we had no thought of seeing. The marvel of marvels is that through infinite grace, we shall be there ourselves.

> I stand upon His merit;
> I know no other stand,
> Not even where glory dwelleth
> In Immanuel's land.

> The Eternal Goodness
> I know not what the future hath
> Of marvel or surprise,
> Assured alone that life and death
> His mercy underlies.

> And so beside the Silent Sea
> I wait the muffled oar;
> No harm from Him can come to me
> On ocean or on shore.

> I know not where His islands lift
> Their fronded palms in air;
> I only know I cannot drift
> Beyond His love and care.

And Thou, O Lord by whom are seen
Thy creatures as they be,
Forgive me if too close I lean
My human heart on Thee!
—*John Greenleaf Whittier* (61–64, 73–80, 85–88)

REWARDS IN HEAVEN

Although, through the grace of God every believer will be in heaven, the further question arises as to whether all the saints are to be on the same level there. Are there to be degrees of position and glory in heaven? All God's people on earth are equal in His sight as far as such a divine relationship is concerned, but they are not equal in respect to gifts, abilities, position, and responsibilities.

If not on earth, how about heaven? Are some of the saints to have different and higher stations than others? There are those who argue against any disparity, affirming that all the people of God are loved by Him with the same love. All are chosen together in Christ, being equally redeemed by His blood and equally interested in the same convent of grace and therefore all are on the same footing in respect to service. To suppose the contrary, it is said, eclipses the glory of divine grace and carries with it the legal idea of being rewarded for our work.

Yet Scripture expressly declares rewards in the hereafter for faithfulness in this world, and these rewards contain nothing inconsistent with the doctrines of grace because those very works, meriting reward, were the effects of God's own operation in and through His servants. In our glorified body, all will be different, for then we shall have a will in perfect accord with God's, a mind as clear as light, a heart with only one passion, a conscience knowing no wrong, and our present faculties perfected with the addition of others of which we have no conception. What a glorious prospect of expansion awaits the child of God—a prospect inspiring us to rest content that "the momentary lightness of tribulation works out for us an eternal, excessively surpassing weight of glory."

Though outwardly we are wasting away, yet inwardly we are being renewed day by day. For our light and momentary troubles are achieving for us an eternal glory that far outweighs them all. So we fix our eyes not on what is seen, but on what is unseen. For what is seen is temporary, but what is unseen is eternal.

(2 Corinthians 4:16–18 NIV)

"Every man's work is to be tried by fire," and the results of such a sifting will determine our place and position in our Lord's governmental control of all things. Thus, rewards are referred to as different *crowns, and we must endeavor by the Spirit to "hold that fast which thou hast, that no man take thy crown"* (Revelation 3:11). A similar warning is given by John when he urges us to *"look to yourselves, that we lose not those things which ye have wrought, but that we receive a full reward"* (2 John 1:8). Many gain a reward, others a full reward. When Paul wrote of the possibility of becoming a castaway (see 1 Corinthians 9:27), He was not referring to his soul but reward for service. The word castaway means rejected or disapproved. The Amplified Bible translates the phrase, *"I myself should become unfit [not stand the test and be unapproved and rejected as a counterfeit]."* Paul was afraid lest, after telling others how to live for Christ, he himself might at last fail so to do, and failing, forfeit the crown he had taught others to win.

No believer can lose his salvation for the simple reason that salvation is not *something* but *Someone*. *"Behold, God is my salvation"* (Isaiah 12:2). Therefore, how can a Christian possibly lose Him? Eternal life is a gift, and once received, becomes the possession of the recipient forever. Recompense at the judgment seat of Christ will not come as a gift but a reward for the way in which we have served the Savior. All the saints at that judgment will inherit heaven, but all within heaven will not have the same capacity, position, or responsibility. One is to have authority over ten cities, and another over only five, according to the use made of opportunity or responsibility here below. (See Luke 19:12–19.) The many references to rewards emphasize the solemn fact that it matters very much how we live and labor here, seeing that the consequences of the same are eternal.

In our Lord's teaching in the parable of the talents (see Matthew 25), He makes it clear that, where there is unequal ability but equal faithfulness, the reward will be the same. In His parable of the pounds, He teaches where there is equal ability but unequal faithfulness, the reward will be graded. While consecrated living and serving bring a certain amount of reward now, the position in glory will be determined at the judgment seat of Christ. (See Matthew 5:12; 1 Corinthians 3:12–15; 2 Corinthians 5:10.) To see a saint occupying a higher position than the one allotted to us will engender no jealousy or dissatisfaction. There will be no discontent among the saints in glory. All are to be satisfied when they awake with His likeness. This does not mean, however, that all are to have the same capacity for enjoying God and heaven, nor that all will have the same privilege of responsibility and authority, nor that all will have the same brightness of glory. (See 1 Corinthians 15:41.) There would be no point at all in promising rewards for loyalty to Christ and His cause if at last all were to share alike. As Dr. J. D. Jones expressed it,

> There are differences in Heaven, differences of attainment and glory. There are some who are scarcely saved (1 Peter 4:18; 1 Corinthians 3:15), and there are some who have an "abundant entrance" into heavenly habitations (2 Peter 1:11). And this fact of difference in attainment is quite compatible with the perfect blessedness of all. Each has all the blessedness he can contain. There is fullness of joy for all, though the capacity for joy may vary in each case.

The recurring promises and also solemn warnings should move us to daily watchfulness, to wholehearted devotion to Christ, and to self-sacrificing service. Your work and mine is to be tried by fire of what "*sort*" it is (1 Corinthians 3:13)—*sort* not *size*. Commendation will be ours, not for the *quantity* of our work but its *quality*. Only those who are "*wise*" are to "*shine as the brightness of the firmament*", and only those who "*turn many to righteousness*" are to shine "*as the stars for ever*" (Daniel 12:3).

When I go down to the grave, I can say I have finished my work; but I cannot say I have finished my life. My tomb is not a blind alley. It is a thoroughfare. It closes in the twilight to open in the dawn.   —*Victor Hugo*

JOY IN HEAVEN

Turning to the positive descriptions of heaven, we find that they are necessarily largely figurative, for human language cannot depict heavenly glories in any other way. In the divine Presence there is ever the "*fullness of joy*" which can enter our hearts even now (Psalm 16:11; 21:6; 36:8; Matthew 25:21, 23). Many of our hymns are taken up with this aspect of heaven. The lines of Ida G. Tremaine are assuring.

> A land of peace without alloy,
> Of joy beyond all earthly joy,
> And naught its calm can e'er destroy.

Our Heavenly Father. Our Father in heaven is the Head of the household. From all eternity it has been His dwelling place. The Lord God, omnipotent and almighty, waits to gather His children home. His finger is on the latch of the door and because He is our loving heavenly Father, we have the assurance of heaven.

> *No one has ever seen God, but God the only Son, who is at the Father's side, has made him known.*   (John 1:18 NIV)

> God, my Father, waiteth there to greet me,
> Child of His delight;
> In the well-beloved Son presented
> Faultless in His sight.

Christ. God's only begotten Son is there and has been from the past eternity. When He became man and lived among men for over thirty-three years, He was homesick for heaven and returned home, taking many with Him, for He made captivity captive. He went back as the Redeemer and Intercessor of the saints and awaits the day when He can descend to the air to take the church to be with Himself.

The Holy Spirit. The Holy Spirit, co-equal and co-existent with the Father and the Son, has shared the same glorious dwelling place. Is the Holy Spirit not the Eternal Spirit? These three, then, the great Trinity in unity, are there in all their magnificent glory.

The Angelic Host. Along with the Father, Son, and Holy Spirit, the vast angelic host will add to the wonder and share in the glory of heaven. Paul speaks of the celestial intelligence as archangels, angels, principalities, powers, thrones, mights, and dominions. (See Romans 8:38; Ephesians 1:20–21; Colossians 1:16, Psalm 103:19–21; Daniel 7:10.) Added to these are the unnamed beings, ten thousand times ten thousand, and thousands of thousands. (See Isaiah 6:2; Hebrew 12:22; Revelation 4:2; 5:11.) Our finite minds cannot comprehend what it means to dwell forever with such an august assembly of holy beings who, with veiled faces, ascribe all honor and majesty to Him, sitting upon the throne.

The Saints. The marvel of marvels is the presence in heaven of the prophets, apostles, martyrs, and saints of all ages, all dear to the heart of the Father because they were redeemed by the blood of His beloved Son. They are not only *"equal unto the angels"* but are round about the throne as *"sons of God, being sons of the resurrection"* (Luke 20:36; Revelation 18:20). Their glorious inheritance was gained by Christ who made them joint-heirs. An heir is one who inherits solely, by himself. A joint-heir is one who inherits with another. Thus, the property and riches of the glory-land will be shared amongst all sinners saved by grace by the Lord Jesus Christ Himself. What a numberless throng of redeemed men, women, and children, all with celestial bodies, will congregate together to live with God forever (Matthew 13:43; Luke 20:35-36; 1 Corinthians 15:48)! In their glorified condition, with bodies changed and made like Christ's glorious body, "the God-consciousness will be supreme in them, holding both soul and body in absolute control, and shredding forth the full power of its glory without hindrance."

> On earth they sought the Savior's grace,
> On earth they loved His name;
> So now they see His blessed face,

And stand before the Lamb:
Singing Glory, glory, glory.
(Anne H. Shepherd, "Around the Throne of God in Heaven," 1815)

ABSENCE OF EVIL, PRESENCE OF GOOD

We now come to the fascinating aspect of the life and work of the saints in heaven. As glorified beings in a timeless world, what knowledge, capabilities, progress, and activities are theirs? How different will life be? Of this we are assured, that its bliss will consist in the absence of those experiences which hinder our perpetual happiness on earth.

No Sickness, Nor Pain. Grateful, as we are for doctors, hospitals, and nurses who help us as we endure the ills the flesh is heir to, it is blessed to know that in the New Jerusalem physical ailments and diseases can never attack the eternal life to which we are heirs. (See Revelation 22:2.)

No Hunger, Nor Thirst. Doubtless the majority of us have never experienced the pangs of hunger. In our affluent society, we have an overabundance. Nevertheless around one in three in less privileged parts of the world live on the borderline of starvation. For the saints among them this promise of full sustenance must be comforting. (See Psalm 36:8; 46:4; Isaiah 49:10; Revelation 7:16–17; 22:1–2.)

No Sorrow, Nor Crying, Nor Tears. Daily, because of sin and separations, an ocean of tears are shed. The death of a friend He loved caused Jesus to weep. In the summer-land above, no eyes are ever wet with tears, for the causes of all tears are forever removed. (See Isaiah 25:8; 35:10; 51:11; 65:19.) God's hand will be the handkerchief to wipe all our grief away.

> He will wipe every tear from their eyes. There will be no more death or mourning or crying or pain, for the old order of things has passed away. (Revelation 21:4 NIV)

No Sea. What separations the sea represents! Watch the heartbreaking farewells as loved ones leave by ship for another land. In

Scriptures, the sea is likewise the emblem of national unrest, turmoil, and turbulence. (See Ecclesiastes 1:7; Isaiah 57:20; Jeremiah 49:23; Revelation 21:1.)

No Death. As soon as a child is born, it commences its pilgrimage to the grave. With war, fearful road fatalities, ravaging diseases, and catastrophes in the realm of nature, death is a busy reaper these days! Heaven is a city without a cemetery. It is the deathless abode of Him who is the Lord of life. (See Hosea 13:14; 1 Corinthians 15:26; Revelation 20:14; 21:4.) The chill of a closed grave is never felt in heaven.

No Sin. We live in a world of sinners lost and ruined by the fall. Sinners by birth, we become sinners by practice. *"For all have sinned and come short of the glory of God"* (Romans 3:23), and sin is the sole primary cause of pain and privation, sickness and sorrow, disease and death. (See also Genesis 3:16–19; Ecclesiastes 2:22–23; Romans 5:12; 8:20–23.) Describing heaven, John said, *"There shall be no more curse"* (Revelation 22:3). The world beyond will never be defiled by a single sin or sinner.

For He must reign until he has put all his enemies under his feet. The last enemy to be destroyed is death. For he "has put everything under His feet."　　　　(1 Corinthians 15:25–27 NIV)

No Night. The Bible uses *night* to illustrate heathen ignorance and profaneness, adversity, death, danger, and robbers who welcome the darkness for their crimes. (See Isaiah 21:12; John 9:6; Romans 13:12; 1 Thessalonians 5:2.) For those who cannot sleep, night is not welcomed. Night can also represent weariness. After a day of honest toil, how weary we are at night. There is no night in heaven and no need of light.

They will see his face, and his name will be on their foreheads. There will be no more night. They will not need the light of a lamp or the light of the sun, for the Lord God will give them light. And they will reign for ever and ever.　　　　(Revelation 22:4–5 NIV)

Rest from Earth's Weary Labor. This does not mean a condition of inactivity throughout eternity, but as Fanny J. Crosby put it,

After the weary conflict
Rest in the Saviour's love;
After the pilgrim journey,
Rest in the Home above.

Unceasing Service. At present, we labor for the Master from the dawn to setting sun. After our earthly service ceases, and we reach heaven, the nature of service will change.

They are before the throne of God and serve him day and night in his temple; and he who sits on the throne will spread his tent over them. Never again will they hunger; never again will they thirst.
(Revelation 7:15–16 NIV)

The throne of God and the Lamb will be in the city, and his servants will serve him. (Revelation 22:3 NIV)

An angel's wing would droop if long at rest,
And God Himself inactive were no longer blessed.
(Carlos Wilcox)

Perfect Knowledge. Because of our finite minds, our knowledge of God and His ways is at best only partial.

Now we are looking in a mirror that gives only a dim, blurred reflection, but then [when perfection comes], we shall see in reality and face to face. (1 Corinthians 13:12 AMP)

With perfect understanding, we shall experience,

New discoveries are made
Of God's unbounded wisdom, power and love,
Which give the understanding larger room
And swell the hymn with ever growing praise.
(Robert Pollock, "The Course of Time")

The Perfection of Safety and Beauty. The great city, the holy Jerusalem, descending out of heaven from God, will have "*walls*" and "*gates*" (suggesting *safety*) and will be covered with gold and "*precious*" stones (indicating *beauty*). (See Revelation 21:1–21.) What a combination this is for our adoring hearts to contemplate:

> True vision of true beauty
> True cure of the distrest,
> Beneath thy contemplation
> Sink heart and voice opprest;
> I know not, oh, I know not
> What joys await us there,
> What radiancy of glory,
> What bliss beyond compare.
> (Robert Pearsall, 1865)

After that, we who are still alive and are left will be caught up together with them in the clouds to meet the Lord in the air. And so we will be with the Lord forever. Therefore encourage each other with these words.   (1 Thessalonians 4:17–18 NIV)

With Dean Alford, we can sing,

> Oh then with raptured greetings,
> On Canaan's happy shore,
> What knitting severed friendship up,
> Where partings are no more!
> Then eyes with joy shall sparkle
> That brimmed with tears of late;
> Orphans no longer fatherless,
> no widows desolate.

CONCLUSION

*"I, Jesus, have sent My angel to testify to you these things for the
churches. I am the root and the descendant of David,
the bright morning star."*
—Revelation 22:16 (NASB)

The apostle John, in the book of Revelation, presents the Lord Jesus as *"the root of David"* and *"the bright morning star."* There is a world of difference between a root and a star, between earth and heaven. John, with perfect unity, blends the matchless character of Jesus as a Root and as a Star, as He reconciles opposite functions within His person.

He is the Shepherd, yet the Lamb; the Priest, yet the Sacrifice; the Vine, yet the Branch; the King, yet the Servant. He Himself tells us that He is the Root and yet the bright and morning Star. There is no natural unity existent between the two. They are utterly unlike each other, yet Christ unites both objects in His own being. Taken separately, the figures are rich in spiritual significance; taken together, they bring encouragement to our hearts. Since He has diversity in Himself, we can find all we need in Him.

Belonging as they do to different worlds, roots and stars suggest that Jesus is a Citizen of both. A root is a common child of earth where the feet of toilers tread, lovers walk, and children play. The star is conspicuous among the glories of the sky. Extreme locations meet in Christ.

Such combination brings hope and comfort to our hearts, seeing that we need the continual assistance of this heavenly-earthly Friend.

We are all like roots. The majority of us have to live out our days in some fixed spot. Some are planted, grow, die, and are buried within the same locality. Days are filled with common duties and the ministries of earth.

Life develops, like a root, amid things of earth. Yet the glory of the commonplace can be ours. Our spirits can shine as stars. We can live in the heavenlies. A radiance not of earth can surround our lives and paths. Some of us are all root—of the earth, earthy. Others are all stars—they live in the clouds. Harmony, however, must reign between roots and stars.

As the Root and Offspring of David, Christ is connected with Israel. He came as the King of the Jews, but was rejected as David's Lord and Heir. Nevertheless He will yet be seen as the promised Messiah.

As the bright and morning Star, Jesus is associated with His church. The morning Star is the harbinger of day. Now from the heights He watches His church toiling against contrary winds, but before long He will come to take His own to the eternal land of light and love.

It was in the fall of 1910. The night was cold and wet as the ocean liner headed for New York in a gale. On board was a veteran missionary returning from seven years of pioneer work in central Africa. He had learned the language, built a school, and organized a small church. As the ship approached the harbor he could hear the faint strains of music, and he wondered, "Have my friends arranged a welcome home reception?"

However, as the ship docked, he was surprised to see a military band in full dress. Alas, they were on duty to welcome the President of the United States, Theodore Roosevelt, who had spent ten months on a safari to central Africa shooting wild animals. No one had met the missionary. He found a cheap hotel room and dried his wet clothes over the small radiator. As he knelt to pray, he said, "Dear Lord, the President is welcomed home with bands and crowds after shooting wild animals. I have served you and my supporters, and no one welcomes me home!" His Master replied, "You are not home yet!"

Until the bright and morning star bursts upon the darkness, let us hitch the little wagons of our lives to Him who is our Star as well as our hidden Root. Then, although we live out our lives as roots of earth, we will yet shine as lights in the world and hereafter as the stars forever.

Sometimes a light surprises
The Christian while he sings;
It is the Lord who rises
With healing in His wings;
When comforts are declining,
He grants the soul again
A season of dear shining
To cheer it after rain.
—*Cowper*

ABOUT THE AUTHOR

When Dr. Herbert Lockyer (1886–1984) was first deciding on a career, he considered becoming an actor. Tall and well-spoken, he seemed a natural for the theater. But the Lord had something better in mind. Instead of the stage, God called Herbert to the pulpit, where, as a pastor, a Bible teacher, and the author of more than fifty books, he touched the hearts and lives of millions of people.

Dr. Lockyer held pastorates in Scotland and England for twenty-five years. As pastor of Leeds Road Baptist Church in Bradford, England, he became a leader in the Keswick Higher Life Movement, which emphasized the significance of living in the fullness of the Holy Spirit. This led to an invitation to speak at the Moody Bible Institute's fiftieth anniversary in 1936. His warm reception at that event led to his ministry in the United States. He received honorary degrees from both the Northwestern Evangelical Seminary and the International Academy of London.

In 1955, he returned to England, where he lived for many years. He then returned to the United States, where he spent the final years of his life in Colorado Springs, Colorado, with his son, the Rev. Herbert Lockyer Jr., a Presbyterian minister who eventually became his editor.

Welcome to Our House!

We Have a Special Gift for You ...

It is our privilege and pleasure to share in your love of Christian classics by publishing books that enrich your life and encourage your faith.

To show our appreciation, we invite you to sign up to receive a specially selected **Reader Appreciation Gift**, with our compliments. Just go to the Web address at the bottom of this page.

God bless you as you seek a deeper walk with Him!

WHITAKER HOUSE